Y0-DFO-875

# FREEDOM
*LIMITED*

# FREEDOM
# *LIMITED*

AN ESSAY ON DEMOCRACY

---

MARTEN TEN HOOR

*Professor of Philosophy and Dean of the College of Arts and Sciences, University of Alabama*

1954

*UNIVERSITY OF ALABAMA PRESS*

Copyright 1954 by University of Alabama Press
Drawer 2877, University, Alabama

Library of Congress Catalogue Number 55-5624

Printed and Bound by Birmingham Printing Company

*To* MARIE M.

*In Vermont, there was embodied in the spirit of the people the conviction that governments were like the houses we live in, made to contribute to human welfare, and that those who lived in them were as free to change and extend the one as they were the other, when the developing needs of the human family called for such alterations and modifications.*

John Dewey

# Preface

MOST MEN ARE INCLINED TO ACCEPT THE GOVERNMENT UNDER which they live much as they do the weather. If the government weather is fine, so to speak, they boast about it; if it is bad, they complain. Under normal conditions, they take their government for granted, ignore it, and go about their private business.

Though it seems a little surprising, this is the natural tendency even of citizens of a democratic state. Except for politicians, who "make" the government, and professors, who think and talk about it, few people are interested in examining the essential nature of their government.

There come times, however, when all but the most indifferent are stirred out of this comfortable acceptance of things as they are. When things go badly wrong—when a serious depression develops, for example—the voters begin asking: What's the matter with our government? Professors and politicians become even more articulate than usual.

Disturbing as it may be, such a domestic crisis does not always stimulate the citizen to undertake a thorough examination of the basic character of his government. The thoughtful citizen is almost driven to this, however, when enemies, internal and external, condemn without qualification the *form* of government itself and advocate its abolishment.

Thought and discussion are likely to be stirred to high temperatures if these enemies, in addition, begin taking practical steps to substitute for it their own form.

The above is more or less the situation in which believers in democracy have found themselves for a generation. Fascism had not merely to be refuted, it had to be defeated. As for communism, it is still daily challenging democracy by word and deed. The natural tendency for the believer in democracy in these circumstances is to point out what is wrong with the enemies who attack him. When the struggle is long continued, however, as it is presently, the attention of the defender is gradually forced on his defenses. The enemy keeps asking embarrassing questions, and the defender discovers that he does not know the answers, although he has always supposed that he did. Or it appears that he is not as sure of them as he thought, or that he cannot state them satisfactorily to himself. There slowly develops in him the need of thinking things through for himself. Why does *he* believe in democracy?

This book is one believer's attempt to answer this question for himself. The need to do this, too, grew out of sustained critical preoccupation with the theories and practices of contemporary enemies of democracy. In the course of attack and refutation, there emerged embarrassing doubts and uncertainties. There was nothing for it but to take an inventory of my own beliefs about democracy.

This book presumes to be no more than that. It is not a textbook, either in political science or philosophy. It is not an "ideology" of democracy, if there be such a thing. Nor is it a complete description of some particular democratic government. It is a combination of "the ideal and the real." I have tried both to identify the essential characteristics of democratic government in theory and to show how and to what extent they are present in reality, that is to say, in a particular democratic state. I naturally selected the democracy with which I am most familiar, namely, the United States of America. In the last analysis, the book is nothing more than a statement of "what democracy means to me." Of course, I thought others might be interested in such a statement, otherwise I would not have offered it for publication.

# PREFACE

Grateful acknowledgments for helpful criticism are due my colleagues, Professors Iredell Jenkins, York Willbern, and James W. Clark. But they bear no responsibility whatever for what I have said in the book. I also wish to thank the Research Committee of the University of Alabama for assistance in typing the manuscript.

One other acknowledgment is due and that is to the editors of the *Algemeen Nederlands Tijdschrift voor Wijsbegeerte en Psychologie*. The greater part of Chapter VI, "The Method of Compromise," appeared in the July, 1950, number of the aforementioned journal, in Dutch translation. I appreciate the editors' permission to use this material in this book.

M. t. H.

## Contents

| | | |
|---|---|---|
| I | INTRODUCTION: FIRST PRINCIPLES | 1 |

*Part One.* THE ENDS OF DEMOCRATIC GOVERNMENT

| | | |
|---|---|---|
| II | PRIVATE ENDS AND CORPORATE ENDS | 11 |
| III | REALIZATION OF ENDS | 19 |
| IV | DEVELOPMENT OF CONFLICTS | 30 |
| V | SETTLEMENT OF CONFLICTS | 43 |
| VI | THE METHOD OF COMPROMISE | 57 |

*Part Two.* THE MACHINERY OF DEMOCRATIC GOVERNMENT

| | | |
|---|---|---|
| VII | THE ROLE OF THE REPRESENTATIVE | 70 |
| VIII | GOVERNMENT BY MAJORITY | 83 |
| IX | THE ROLE OF THE MINORITY | 95 |

*Part Three.* THE DEMOCRATIC CITIZEN AND THE DEMOCRATIC STATE

| | | |
|---|---|---|
| X | THE PRIMACY OF THE INDIVIDUAL | 109 |
| XI | COOPERATIVE LIMITATION OF FREEDOM | 123 |
| XII | WHERE FREEDOM ENDS | 136 |

*Part Four.* THE OUTLOOK FOR DEMOCRACY

| | | |
|---|---|---|
| XIII | THE DEMOCRATIC VIRTUES | 153 |
| XIV | THE WEAKNESSES OF DEMOCRACY | 165 |
| XV | A TRIAL BALANCE | 184 |
| XVI | THE FUTURE OF DEMOCRACY | 205 |

*ONE*

# Introduction: First Principles

MOST MEN WILL AGREE THAT THE PURPOSE OF ANY GOVERNMENT is the promotion of the good of the governed. An absolute monarch may in actual practice do very little for his subjects; unless he is a fool as well as a tyrant he will nevertheless publicly maintain that he has only their welfare at heart. An autocrat may actually be leading his people straight toward destruction, as Hitler did; in his own mind he will think that he is leading them, or their descendants, towards some glorious future! There are those who believe that it is the function of a government to execute the will of God; surely neither those who govern nor those who are governed will maintain that God intends anything but the good of his creatures. The Communist is convinced, to the point of fanaticism, that his form of government (and no other) will assure justice and security to all men. Such terms as "the common good" and "the public welfare" occur in every constitution, in every speech from the throne, and in every manifesto. It cannot rightly be maintained, therefore, that democracy is the only form of government that is a government "for the people."

Nor is it the only form of government that claims to be dedicated to the good of *all* the people. In a general sense, almost all governments profess this. When Alexander the Great attempted to introduce elements of Greek culture into the countries which he had conquered, he was convinced that this would bring about an improvement in the native cultures. The monarchs of the Holy Roman Empire claimed that they were the personal secular representatives of God and therefore knew what was best for all men and were justified in extending the scope of their imperial authority accordingly. In our day, proponents of communism have bettered the claim of supporters of democracy by promising that their form of government (and no other) will assure the realization of the good of *all* mankind *for all time*. Other historic parties and personalities with ambitions to rule the world have had notions of this kind.

In view of the fact that the conceptions of the common good to which such governments were committed were so varied, agreement on the general principle actually meant very little. In the opinion of believers in democracy, some of these rulers and governments seemed to intend the opposite of the common good. There was, for example, the claim that some men were born to be slaves and that therefore it was a friendly accommodation on the part of the rulers to keep them so. Minorities were oppressed, persecuted, and eliminated for reasons of religion, race, or politics on the ground that such disciplinary measures, when they were fatal, were for the good of the survivors, and when they were not, for the good of the victims. Attempts to establish a world government such as the Pan-German program of National Socialism were actually nothing but attempts to reduce the greater part of mankind to a state of servitude.

It will be noted that in all these examples the nature of the common good, however it may be conceived, is determined by those who govern and not by those who are governed. In the area of world government, the Holy Roman emperor claimed this was his privilege by divine right. The hereditary monarch claimed the right to govern by virtue of his royal descent. In Nazi Germany, Hitler claimed this right because of an intuitive certainty that he represented the most complete and most perfect concentration of the spirit of the German race. In the U.S.S.R. the Politburo, supported by approximately six million members of the Communist Party, bases its right to govern the other 200 million citizens on its accurate knowledge of the course which human history is going to take. In each of the above forms of government, those who are governed, although they are supposed to be the ultimate beneficiaries, have only the duty of acceptance and obedience.

It is with respect to this basic characteristic that democracy differs from all other forms of government. Democracy maintains that those who are governed and not those who govern must in the last analysis have the right to determine what is good for the governed. Democracy believes in *self*-government. In common with all decent governments, it assumes that the promotion of the good of the governed is the primary purpose of government. But it further insists that if government is to be *"for* the people" it must be *"by* the people." If the purpose of laws and taxes is to benefit the people, the people should be allowed to determine what benefits are desired. No one has a better right to this, because no one knows better what they want and need.

To be sure, there are always individuals or groups of individuals who claim to know better. Their claim, however, rests on their own judgment. There is no reason why other men should automatically accept this judgment. The claim to know better what is good for others than the others themselves know has no authority as such. The validity of this claim must be judged by those who are to experience the consequences. We are all human beings. No man is God. If a man claims to speak for God, as does the king who claims to rule by divine right, his claim must be believed by his subjects or they will not recognize his authority. The ruler's own judgment that he has been designated to rule is not enough. If a "fuehrer" claims to be the most complete and perfect embodiment of his race or his nation, the claim will be an empty one if his race or his nation does not recognize and accept him as such. If a claimant to authority over his fellowmen bases his claim on superior knowledge of the ultimate destiny of man, such a prophet—for he *is* a prophet—will not be honored in his own fatherland unless the people grant him superior knowledge. There is no alternative to human judgment. To insist that the original source is superhuman is no escape, for the alleged superhuman judgment must pass through a human consciousness. A human being is the medium of communication to other human beings. If other human beings accept a communication alleged to come from a superhuman source, it is because they believe that it is genuine and that the deliverer is trustworthy. In the last analysis, popular acceptance of the authority of the claimant thus becomes the real determinant of authority.

From the two propositions that the government must promote the good of the governed and that the governed must have the right to determine the nature of the good, it follows that the governed should determine the policies of the government. It is obvious that the governed cannot do this *in person*. In any democratic nation there are too many of them. Imagine all the citizens of the United States marching periodically to Washington to make the nation's laws! Self-government in person is possible only in local units and then only when the body of voters is small in number, as is the case in the New England town-meeting. When the body of voters is large, representative government in the democratic sense is the solution.

Before there can be self-government by voters through their representatives, there must be a government. No government, no matter of what form, falls from heaven ready-made; it must be established by human beings. To be completely consistent, a democratic government ought to be established by those for whom the government is intended. Here again it is not practicable for all the people who are interested in forming a democratic government to participate in its founding. Representatives must be selected whose responsibility it will be to lay down fundamental principles and select political procedures. These "founding fathers" are the authors of the "basic documents": declarations of principles, articles of confederation, and constitutions. Such documents are the first representative expression of the will of the people and that is why they become the basic law of the land. They state, directly or by implication, the beliefs and convictions to which the government is committed; for example, such convictions as have been discussed above, namely, that the government must promote the good of the governed and that the governed must have the right to determine the nature of the good. More specifically, they define the respective rights and duties of the citizens and of the governing officials.

But a constitution must do more than this. To be practical, it must provide for workable political procedures. The good, whether private or public, is not brought into being by the declaration of principles. A constitution must provide political machinery for the accomplishment of its purposes. In a democracy, the most important practical problem is the provision of political machinery which can be depended upon not only to make but also to keep the actual conduct of the government representative. This is the purpose of general suffrage and periodic elections. These procedures make it possible for *all* the citizens to participate in the selection of government officials. In the pre-governing stage of party politics, the voters can also elect their party leaders and thus see to it that these leaders also are representative. In this fashion, the voters can, to a considerable extent, determine the principles of their political party and thus indirectly the policies of the government. To be sure, neither voters nor parties nor government officials are absolutely free. All must operate within the limits of the constitution, both with respect to political principles and practices.

Elected representatives do not become free agents, however, by virtue of their election. The citizens have effective ways of controlling them between elections. There are pressure groups, with agents and agencies operating in politically strategic locations, by means of which contact is maintained with elected and appointed officials of the government. There is also the potent and ubiquitous influence of public opinion. By way of the press and the radio, which in a democracy must and can be free, the public is immediately informed of what public officials are doing. The voters are often fairly well informed even on the intentions of their representatives.

Modern means of communication have made these informal and indirect controls very efficient and powerful. Whereas only a few decades ago it might be weeks after the fact that a citizen in a remote section of the United States would read or hear of the passage of some law by which his life would be seriously affected, today his radio informs him as soon as it is proposed. As a result, he can also, if he wishes, immediately communicate his opinions to his representatives. Members of the Congress of the United States are often flooded with telegrams as soon as their positions on some important issue become known. Government officials and politicians, on their part, have developed their own machinery and techniques for informing themselves of the state of public opinion. As the saying has it, they "keep their ear to the ground." The result of this greater sensitivity has been a greater sense of responsibility of the representatives to the citizens.

\* \* \*

The unique machinery of democracy has a second fundamental purpose: periodic elections make it possible, and fairly easy, for the voters to bring about changes in the government. Such changes may be necessary in order to correct mistakes. Some representatives may turn out to be *un*-representative. Others may have misunderstood the will of the people or have decided to ignore it. An official of the government may have taken the bit in his teeth and devised and initiated a new and unacceptable policy. The machinery intended to make government representative would only be half effective if it functioned only at election time.

But it is not only representatives and public officials who change: the external circumstances under which the voters live do not remain the same. An economic depression is a good example of a change in internal conditions and a foreign war of a change in external circumstances. There may even be permanent though gradual internal changes, as, for example, from the simple and independent life of people on the frontier to the complex and highly dependent life of people living in large cities. The economy of a country or of a section of the country may be gradually changing from a predominantly agricultural to a predominantly industrial character. When the conditions of life change, there must be a corresponding change in social processes and social institutions. Such changes must be reflected by changes in the policies, and sometimes even in the machinery of government.

*First Principles* 7

Changes in the external conditions of life are not the only occasion for changes in government. It is true that the external conditions under which human beings live are often the cause of such change. With new environmental conditions come new needs, desires, and interests. But people also change simply as people. Sometimes the voters change for strictly private reasons: the influences seem to be wholly within the consciousness of the individual. There are, for examples, changes in religious beliefs, in conceptions of individual rights, in the sense of public duty, in degree of interest in property. Such changes, individually or in combination, are almost certain to bring about important changes in the conception of both private and public welfare. Men come to expect or demand more or less from their government; they change their politics —and vote accordingly.

Finally, there are changes in the processes of government, the occasions for which lie within the government itself. The need for these changes is indicated by the way the government is "working." Men learn to do better what they are already doing reasonably well. Some changes are frequently recommended by officials of the government; sometimes they are insisted upon by the voters. Administrative reorganization involving the creation or combination or abolishment of offices is a good example of conscious change initiated by professional or lay experts in governmental efficiency. When they are in the direction of expansion and increased complexity, changes in the organization of government sometimes develop of their own momentum. Thus bureaus create problems which require more bureaus—and more bureaucrats—to solve them. Changes in governmental process and organization frequently occur during periods of the greatest stability. They represent a normal accumulation of social experience, specifically, of experience in the business of governing.

That men can—and must—learn to govern better is an implicit assumption of the democratic *ideal* of government. To be responsive to what has been learned is an important potential of the democratic *form* of government. In a democracy, what has been learned can be promptly put into effect. The voters are never finally committed to a decision, and thus to a possible mistake. Capacity for change is inherent in the democratic process itself. The constitutional prescription of elections at stated intervals and regular times provides the voters with opportunity and means to effect changes in the policies and procedures of government. In cases of emergency, the referendum is available for an urgent pronouncement on policies and the power of impeachment for the dismissal of unrepresentative officials.

To be sure, other forms of government have capacity for change. What constitutes the great advantage of democracy is that changes can be effected by means of processes native to itself and prescribed by its own constitution. The democratic form of government is *self-corrective.* In a democracy, change can therefore be effected by *peaceful* and *orderly* means. Too much emphasis cannot be laid on the terms 'peaceful' and 'orderly.' The only alternative to change by peaceful and orderly means is change by force, that is, by revolution. Since in a democracy there is no entrenched power to be overthrown, there is no need for a revolution to overthrow it. The government needs only to be voted out of office. It did not gain office by force; it does not maintain itself in office by force; therefore, force is not necessary to put it out of office. In a democracy, advocacy of revolution cannot be justified as long as democratic processes are in effect. The citizen of a democracy has no need for the assassin's bomb: he has the vote.

The democratic way is not only the peaceful and orderly way to effect political change; it is also the most efficient way. Revolutions destroy; democratic procedures reform. The lives and material resources which are sacrificed in the overthrow of an autocratic government would, in even the most drastic democratic upheaval, be conserved for a better life and for wiser use. Moreover, since it is in the nature of a revolution to go too far and thus force a change to the other extreme, a long period of correction is required before the real purpose of the revolution is accomplished. Revolutions usually suppress, temporarily if not permanently, the liberties which they are intended to restore. Finally, the logical answer to a revolution is another revolution. The consequences of a revolution breed the need and occasion for another. Men become revolution-minded and gradually become politically conditioned to think and feel and act as revolutionaries. Examples are to be found in the history of certain South American republics. Although the "revolutionary" character of this history, in contrast with the peaceful internal life of western democracies, cannot properly be wholly ascribed to difference in form of government, it is undoubtedly in large part due to the habit of thinking of revolution as the necessary means of effecting political change.

* * *

The capacity for self-correction, the second essential characteristic of the democratic form of government, is complementary to the other essential characteristic, representativeness, and greatly extends its scope and power. It provides the voters with the means for keeping the government permanently representative. Negatively considered, the purpose of the self-corrective machinery of democracy may be defined as (a) the prevention of a final commitment by any political administration to any particular set of social or economic policies, and (b) the prevention of the entrenchment in power of any individual, family, social class, economic group, or political party. The positive purpose is to keep the citizens in control of the government. To the abolishment or neutralization of this means of self-correction the believer in democracy must therefore be unalterably opposed. Such a change would alter the essential nature of democracy and sooner or later bring about its destruction.

The two essential characteristics, representativeness and self-correction, in combination, constitute the means of control of the policies and personnel of democratic government by the citizens. By their proper and steady use, the citizens can make sure that the government will be devoted to the promotion of their common good as they themselves conceive this. These characteristics may therefore be said to identify the unique nature of a democratic form of government. Imposing as they may sound, they are only general ideas, however, and they do not tell us much about the inner workings of democracy. General ideas are like broad promises: they are assuring but they are not enlightening. No sensible person will wish finally to commit himself to a particular form of government on the strength of generalities; for such commitment means the acceptance of control over a great part of one's life. Faith and loyalty require firmer grounds. They require a clear understanding of the implications of these general characteristics.

They demand an answer to several specific questions about the theory and practice of democratic government. Exactly what is meant by the common good? How is the common welfare of a hundred million people or more to be determined? How can a single government possibly promote the common welfare of so many people? What is to be done if the citizens, or their representatives, have conflicting ideas about this? Over what interests and activities of the citizens should the government have control? Can the great mass of people who constitute the citizenry be expected to know enough to determine the domestic and foreign policies of the government? How can a form of government which provides for such frequent changes in policy and personnel have any stability? Can such a form of government survive? To these and other equally practical questions, the student of government will wish to have an answer before passing judgment on the advantages and disadvantages of democracy as compared with other forms of government.

PART I  THE ENDS OF DEMOCRATIC
GOVERNMENT

*TWO*

## Private Ends and Corporate Ends

THE FUNCTION OF A DEMOCRATIC FORM OF GOVERNMENT, LIKE that of any good government, is the promotion of the common good of the citizens, but with the unique proviso that the citizens themselves are to determine its nature. Every citizen who votes plays a part in this. The common good which the government is to promote therefore represents the general opinion of the citizens. The notion of the common good has its origin in the hearts and minds of the people. This is true both for original declarations in basic documents such as the constitution and for interpretation of and amendments to these declarations. The purpose of the government therefore represents a common end or purpose of the citizens. The processes of democracy are the means by which the citizens seek to promote this common end. The end of a democratic form of government can therefore be restated as the promotion of the greatest possible realization of the ends of the citizens.

Upon first consideration, this statement seems somewhat confusing. It refers to a common end, that is, the end of the government, and also to the ends of all the citizens. For purposes of identification let us call the end of the government a *corporate* end and the individual ends of the citizens *private* ends. What is the relation between the corporate end and the private ends? Is the corporate end merely a kind of arithmetical sum of the private ends? Or does the corporate end represent only those private ends which the citizens have in common, it being assumed that there are, in addition, other private ends with which the government is in no way concerned?

The answer to these questions is to be found in the basic democratic doctrine that the corporate end is a *means* by which the citizens cooperatively promote their private ends. A form of government is a social institution devised by men for the purpose of cooperative living. The notion to cooperate was born out of the desire of individuals for a more effective way of realizing their own purposes. The corporate end is not an end in itself: it is merely a means to an end. Institutions are social agencies for the realization of corporate ends. The family, the club, the lodge, the church, the school, and the government are agencies for the promotion of group or corporate ends. A form of government is merely a cooperative way of living, a working together for the good of all, a corporate way of promoting private purposes which the citizens have in common.

All this implies that individuals existed before institutions and that private ends existed before corporate ends. Corporate ends may be said to emerge out of private ends. The processes of this emergence are varied and complex. Something of the nature of these processes is suggested if we introduce the notion of levels of ends and imagine these to be arranged in an order which simulates the evolution of the institution of political government out of the independent and unorganized "private" lives of individuals. Human beings have a variety of private needs, desires, and interests; for example, need for food, desire for comfort, interest in sports. Some of these needs, desires, and interests are inborn; some are acquired in the course of life. The satisfactions of these needs, desires, and interests are the ends or purposes of life.

On the first level, each individual is interested only in the promotion of his personal ends. His ends are not only private; they are also independent of each other. The ends do not take each other into consideration, so to speak. The individual tries to satisfy each particular need and desire and interest as it occurs, without relation to or consideration of the need and opportunity for satisfaction of any other. Not only the individual as a whole but each of the ends is "selfish." If he wants food, he indulges himself, even though it makes him ill or unfits him for the chase. If he desires to possess some thing, he simply takes it, though it brings him the dangerous enmity of his neighbor. He is the creature of his impulses: undisciplined, unreflective, unorganized, and hardly worthy of the name human being.

On the second level, the individual brings some system into the business of attaining his ends. He establishes a kind of order and balance among them, so that the satisfaction of one need, desire, or interest will not interfere with the satisfaction of another. As we say, he learns to "control his impulses." For example, he limits his eating and drinking so that he may be fit for a long journey, for a strenuous hunt, or for battle. He reduces his leisure in order to improve his living conditions. He denies himself pleasures in order to please his god. He may even come to the point of aiming all his activities, or all that seem necessary, at the realization of a single dominating end, for example, the attainment of a chiefhood, or a place in heaven. This end gives his whole life plan and meaning. Out of an unorganized and disorderly mass of impulses and instincts, there has emerged an organized whole, a personality. He becomes a *rational* human being, at least in part.

His life is still strictly private and independent, however; and it remains so until he discovers that he can better realize his own ends in cooperation with his fellows. On the third level he learns, for example, that he can more quickly and easily obtain food on the hunt if he hunts in company with his neighbors. He and his fellows both profit when they join hands in building their huts, in meeting emergencies such as putting out a fire, and in many other kinds of activities. It should, of course, not be forgotten that the need for love and affection, the desire for "company" and friendship, the liking for commendation and honor, and the satisfaction experienced in working or playing together and in helping others require cooperation for their satisfaction and are thus strong motivating forces on this level. Nevertheless, cooperation with others on this level is only occasional and temporary.

When men realize that their need for cooperation is enduring, they found institutions. An institution provides machinery for regular and efficient cooperation between its members. This fourth level is the level of non-political institutions, institutions concerned, for example, with the promotion of social, religious, economic, educational, and artistic ends. Such institutions vary in character from those in which membership is in part involuntary to those in which it is entirely voluntary. A child is born into a family involuntarily and remains a biological member of it though he may eventually sever all other connections with it. On the other hand, membership in a social club or fraternal order or church may be wholly a matter of deliberate choice.

The membership of an individual in an organization or institution implies commitment to the common purposes of all or a majority of the members of the group. The ends of institutions are therefore corporate ends. In so far as their corporate ends are concerned, the members constitute a *corpus*, a single body, and undertake to act as one. The ends of the members have become "institutionalized." Ideally, it becomes the aim and duty of every member to promote the welfare of the institution and to accept its authority as a means to the realization of the corporate ends. To be sure, this does not mean that the members do not have other ends, either as represented by membership in other institutions or strictly private ends. For example, a man may at the same time belong to a church, a fraternal order, a social club, a choral society, and a business organization without any resultant conflict between his several commitments and loyalties. However, membership in an institution implies, ideally at least, that there shall be no conflict between the corporate end of the institution of which the individual is a member and his other ends. It is obvious that membership in an institution helps to introduce order and consistency into the life of the individual.

On the fifth level, men seek to promote the realization of their ends through the medium of political institutions, namely governments. The political state is a complex and highly organized institution whose corporate end is the promotion of the good of the governed through the machinery of government. It is to some extent a super-institution; for its corporate end is not only the promotion of the ends of the citizens as individuals but also of the various non-political institutions into which the citizens are organized. A democratic state such as the United States of America thus lies on the fifth level. Although this study is concerned with government as limited to a single state or nation, it should be noted that the idea of institutionalization can be extended to provide for a super-state, a political, racial, or religious world-state, which could be considered a sixth level, at least in respect to extent. The corporate end of such a world-state, conceived in terms of the world today, would be the promotion of the common ends of the member states.

*  *  *

The corporate end of a democratic form of government has been defined as the promotion of the greatest possible realization of the ends of the citizens. This does not mean that the other four levels of activity are eliminated or completely absorbed. The democratic state does not undertake to replace the individual and his non-political institutions completely. On the contrary, it also undertakes to protect the rights of the citizens to live their own lives as individuals and as groups and to promote their own private and institutional ends. What now is the relation between the activities of the state on the fifth level and the activities of individuals and groups on the other four levels? Exactly what relation is there between the corporate end and the private ends of individuals and of institutions?

The first and most fundamental point to be made is this: since a government is established by the prospective citizens for the purpose of promoting their private ends by means of cooperative activity, the private ends of the citizens are the original or direct ends and the corporate end is a derived or indirect end. There would be no occasion for a corporate end if there were no private ends, for there is no need for a "means" if there is no "end." There would be no need for a state, if there were no prospective citizens. The state, like any institution, grows out of the needs, desires, and interests of its members.

Secondly, it must not be assumed that because these ends are private they are necessarily selfish and that, in consequence, the citizen of a democracy can have no interest in the welfare of his fellowmen. This assumption is the result of the failure to distinguish between the notions "selfish" and "self-motivated." Even unselfish motives are the motives of an individual and thus of a self. Unselfish motives are not disembodied or depersonalized motives; they do not float about in the air outside of persons. If A wishes to assist neighbor B in building a house, it is A who has the interest and who feels the urge. The love which the mother feels for her child is *her* love, not that of some other mother. The interests which a democratic government undertakes to promote are the private ends of the citizens, no matter whether these ends are "selfish" or "unselfish."

Finally, the establishment of a government for the purpose of promoting a corporate end does not imply the discontinuance of all private promotion of ends. Individuals may have the same interest and yet have no desire to cooperate in the promotion of this interest. Some men insist on attending to their own philanthropies, for example. These individuals have an unselfish interest in common but they do not have a corporate interest. The citizens of a democracy do not turn over to the government the responsibility for the promotion of all their private ends. On the contrary, they resent it if someone even proposes this, or if the government shows a tendency to assume responsibility for the promotion of some ends without their permission. They are quite willing that the government shall deliver the mail, but they resent it if the government undertakes to tell them what magazines they must read. It is of the essence of democracy for the citizens to claim the right to decide what private ends the corporate end is to embrace and to insist on retaining this right. That is why the government is *their* government.

The retention by the citizens of the right to the private promotion of some ends seems to imply that, with respect to these ends, the government has no other function but the negative one of non-interference. A moment's reflection will reveal that this is an unrealistic assumption. Private citizens and institutions depend to a great extent on the government for the maintenance of the opportunity to promote their private ends. Initial non-interference by the government in the area of private ends is no guarantee of non-interference by the citizens and private institutions with one another. For this reason the citizens assign to their government much of the responsibility for protection against such interference. The government forbids a man to interfere with the private life of his neighbor and punishes him, i.e. interferes, if he does so. This "police" function is an important part of the corporate end of government. The citizens also depend on the government for a more positive contribution: they expect the government to create and maintain favorable conditions for the pursuit of private ends. Citizens who live in an area which is subject to floods are likely to expect the government to assume responsibility for flood control. Farmers not only expect the government to deliver the mail but are also likely to expect it to maintain the roads so that they may be able to bring their products to market.

It is thus the business of democratic government to promote the ends of the citizens and *as the citizens conceive them.* The corporate end must therefore be kept *transparent:* the good of the citizens must always be "visible through" the corporate end. The governing authorities must always keep the ends of the citizens in mind. If this is not done, the government is likely to develop independent ends of its own and thus lose its reason for existence. Government will become an end in itself. To permit the government to develop independent ends of its own is to accept the doctrine that the citizens exist for the benefit of the state instead of the reverse.

The believer in democracy can therefore not accept the doctrine that the corporate end of the state is imposed on the citizens *from the outside.* The claim of German National Socialism that the corporate end of the state is imposed on the state by the genius of the race, the doctrine that a king receives his authority and instructions directly from God, the

Communist dogma that the government is a means for the realization of a dialectical purpose innate in matter, are all unacceptable to the believer in democracy. For him, the state is simply an institution organized by individuals for the promotion of their own ends. That is why the corporate end of the state can correctly be said to derive its authority from the citizens.

*THREE*

# Realization of Ends

THE GREATEST POSSIBLE REALIZATION OF THE ENDS OF THE citizens must therefore be the aim of a democratic government. The state must help the citizens to live rich, satisfying, useful lives. Self-realization for the citizens—not for the state—is the ultimate goal. Needless to say, this is a difficult task. As a matter of fact, no form of government undertakes to do as much. Every individual knows how difficult it is to organize his own life so that he will attain the most complete and lasting satisfaction of his own interests. The more numerous and insistent the demands, the more difficult is the attempt to satisfy them. An individual, however, is to some extent concerned only with his own ends; the state must be concerned with all the ends of all the citizens. It must therefore also be concerned with the purposes of the non-political organizations and institutions which men have established to promote the private ends which they have in common. Both individuals and non-political institutions make demands upon the government for the inclusion of private ends in the corporate end of the state. To what extent can these demands be satisfied? How can this be done in orderly and peaceful fashion?

Before such questions can be adequately answered, it is necessary to determine the general possibilities and conditions for the realization of human ends. In general the possibility of the attainment of any end and of the degree of its attainment depends on three factors: (1) the nature of the specific end, both with respect to quality and quantity; (2) the nature of other ends in the same individual or group, or in other individuals or groups; (3) the character of the setting or environment in which the ends are pursued.

That the quality or character of an end may itself preclude the possibility of realization is illustrated by the case of the child's desire for the moon, the desire to live forever and the search for a method of squaring the circle. Such ends can hardly be considered rational, and they are not usually entertained by normal mature human beings. An end may likewise be impossible of realization because of the quantity of degree of attainment which is desired. The possession of *all* knowledge, the acquisition of *all* the property in the world, political dominance over *all* men are ends which in point of quantity are so extreme as to be irrational. For adults to entertain them is usually considered a symptom of mental disturbance. The ends of organizations and institutions are occasionally quite as unreasonable as these eccentric individual ends. We have but to recall the German National Socialist dream of world conquest. Fanaticism, extremism, and even a mild unreasonableness in demand for realization may make any degree of realization impossible. Desire and ambition, when they overreach themselves, may attain annihilation instead of realization.

Although we may speak loosely of a normal range of possible realization of an end, it is not possible to determine the limits solely in terms of the end itself. For a desire, need, or interest does not appear in a vacuum; it is an element of a personality. An end, even when it is all-pervasive and dominant, appears in association with other ends. The possibility and desirability of the realization of any single end are limited by the qualitative and quantitative character of other ends. No matter how great his particular ambition, a man, if he is to live at all, must give some attention to other ends; for example, to health and security. No personality is constituted solely of ambition, of lust for power, of desire for knowledge, of hope of salvation, or of brotherly love. Life for every normal human being is a complex of interests and activities. The realization of the ends of any individual is limited by this multiplicity and complexity. The need of organization is therefore a foregone conclusion.

The same is true for an institution, though in this case the difficulty of organization is usually not so great. Since the members have combined in order to accomplish some specific purpose, the aim of the institution is selective and limited. Other interests are by common consent ignored. Singleness of purpose gives an institution singleness of direction. A labor union, for example, may be interested only in establishing higher wages. There could scarcely be greater unanimity of purpose and more effective cooperative action than that exemplified in a chess club. To be sure, the more numerous or complex the purposes of the institution, the more difficult it is to establish order among them. It is much more difficult to construct a platform of action for a political party than for a manufacturers' association. If a religious institution undertakes to enter into politics, it is likely that the unanimity of opinion on religious issues will be disturbed and effectiveness in the area of religious life be reduced. The fortunes and the life span of an institution are to some extent determined by singleness of purpose or the lack of it. History reveals that disputes and schisms are often more common in religious denominations whose doctrines are complex and involved as well as rigid, than in the case of those whose doctrines are vague, superficial, and generally comfortable.

In addition to these internal limitations present to the individual or institution there are external limitations to the realization of ends. The efforts of an individual to realize his needs, desires, and interests are limited by the efforts of other individuals to do the same thing for their ends. Even the most balanced individual and the best organized institution may be opposed or embarrassed in attempts at realization by other individuals and institutions. In his efforts to acquire wealth, A is limited by B and C, who also desire wealth and who may want as much or more of it than A does. Even the strongest political candidate does not have the field to himself; if he seems too strong, his opponents may even combine against him. The ambitious person has to reckon with other persons equally ambitious. For every talent there is likely to be a talent equally great, or greater, which may offer competition. Even if there were "enough realization to go around" it is not likely that a satisfactory division could be effected, or maintained.

In the case of institutions, the same social problem exists. When an organization is formed for some specific purpose, almost certainly other individuals will form an organization whose aim it is to oppose this purpose or to promote it in a different and allegedly more promising way. There are certain natural tendencies in the realm of institutional life with which everyone is familiar. Subordinates are inclined to organize "against" their superiors. When superiors are too hard pressed by these organizations, they themselves form a protective organization. Promiscuously competing interests combine against common "enemies." Thus rival organizations of employees may bury their differences and unite against organizations of employers.

Every individual, unless he is a hermit, and every institution, must these days function in a highly organized society. This society is a third factor to be considered in the problem of the realization of ends. Society often delimits and sometimes prevents the realization of individual and institutional ends. It also frequently promotes such realization. When the social environment is favorable, the organization of society actually increases opportunities for the satisfaction of needs, desires, and interests, or improves the quality of such opportunities. To be sure, it usually insists on doing this in its own way and consequently demands conformance and cooperation. Whatever the social situation, both individuals and institutions must adjust themselves to it or accept the consequences.

Individuals and institutions pursue their ends not only in a social environment but also in a physical environment. Just as the farmer's success is to some extent limited by the productivity of his land, so individuals and institutions are limited in the realization of their ends by the potentialities of their physical home. The character of the soil, the topography of the land, the presence or absence of natural means of transportation, the amount and degree of availability of mineral resources, these are some of the factors that determine to what extent individuals and institutions can expect to satisfy their needs, desires, and interests.

They also determine to what extent they are dependent on one another. The more limited the resources, the more dependent an individual or nation is on other individuals or nations. The distribution of resources determines the relative importance of their possession or control. In a country with limited oil fields but extensive forests, the ownership of oil is likely to be a source of greater power and influence than the ownership of lumber. The natural tendency of exclusive possession to strengthen individualistic traits in the possessor—for example, to encourage his sense of independence and even to breed arrogance and pride—is likely to create obstacles to the realization of ends on the part of others. Scarcity of necessary goods will invariably intensify competition for their possession. Thus the character of the physical environment may tend to develop or encourage anti-social tendencies and create an unfavorable socio-psychological environment for cooperative effort.

It may, on the other hand, do exactly the opposite. When men become conscious of these anti-social tendencies and clearly see their undesirable consequences, they may be influenced to greater cooperation. Those who possess the least are sometimes the most generous. The obvious dangers of great economic inequality and of over-concentration of power sometimes encourage men to seek a cooperative way of escape. The common problems created by anti-social tendencies lead sensible men to inquire into the causes of these tendencies and to search for means of correction or amelioration. However, even with the best of will, men cannot escape all the limitations of their physical environment but must content themselves with consequent limitations in the realization of their ends.

In the case of both individuals and organizations, the complexity and multiplicity of ends require some kind and degree of organization among them. Lack of such organization in the individual results in confused and disorderly living; in sensitive personalities such disorder may cause pathological conditions which are difficult to correct. An organization or institution likewise must organize its purposes if it is to have order in its activities. A society made up of a variety of organizations must establish and maintain order among them if it is to be a peaceful and stable society. In each case we have the problem of the relation of private ends to corporate ends. The varied needs, desires, and interests of an individual must be organized into a life purpose, which will be the integrated end of the whole personality. An organization would not be worthy of the name if it did not have an organizational, that is, "corporate" purpose. The terms society, state, and nation imply that the constituent elements have a common purpose, a "corporate" end.

* * *

The establishment of a corporate end by means of organization obviously involves the limitation of ends. The character and degree of limitation that are necessary will depend to a large extent on the "native" character of the ends and of the "natural" relations between them. Ends may be classified from the point of view of their interrelations as tending by nature to be indifferent, cooperative, or conflicting. Some needs, desires, and interests are in character mutually independent and do not interfere with one another, though it may not be possible to satisfy them at the same time. A man can pursue a hobby without neglecting his business or profession. Each man can cultivate his own garden and grow what he pleases, happily occupied with his own work and content with its results. He can satisfy a moderate desire for knowledge and a moderate desire for money without even the risk of conflict between them. The desire for good health in one man can be completely satisfied without necessarily involving the same desire in his neighbor. Men can worship their own gods in various ways, individually or in association with their fellows, without disturbance or friction. Especially in the realm of imagination and thought, man can develop and maintain a rare degree of privacy and independence. Countless numbers of men and women spend a substantial part of their lives in the peaceful and private pursuit of such ends, without external direction and control and without friction or conflict with their fellows.

These ends cannot be depended upon automatically to

maintain this happy relationship, however. The "native" independent character of the ends is not a permanent guarantee of absence of conflict or need of control. This character is easily altered by external circumstances. There is the classic example of shipwrecked men whose normally friendly attitude is transformed into deadly enmity under the pressure of hunger. Internal dispositions of men are changed by external circumstances. If the latter are unfavorable, men disagree and quarrel, and sometimes fight, over interests which would be wholly independent under more favorable conditions. Thus in times of war men may condemn, and even purposely destroy, those art-works of the enemy which in time of peace they admired and cherished.

Men thus have a common interest in the creation and maintenance of an environment which is favorable to the pursuit of private ends. This common interest is represented in the corporate end of an organization or institution. One of the functions of the government with respect to independent ends is to provide an environment which is hospitable to the realization of these ends. The citizens expect the government to encourage the pursuit of these ends. The provision of a public library is usually considered a proper function of the government. The subsidization of symphony orchestras is by some considered a responsibility of local, state, or even federal government, not because it is considered the proper and normal responsibility of government to provide employment for musicians but because such subsidization provides or increases the opportunity for the citizens to hear good music.

A second class of ends are those which are "naturally" cooperative. A fondness for singing disposes the individual to sing with others who are likeminded. A fondness for games requires the cooperation of others for its satisfaction. The education of children is more efficiently managed by means of a jointly supported school than by means of private arrangements. When the insistence upon group education is based upon a desire to instill common principles and to train for a uniform way of life, the educational institution is an even better example of the promotion of ends which are, to begin with, harmonious and cooperative.

Every institution is a proof of the existence of such ends. In the case of government, the scope of agreement is, at least in some cases, nation-wide. Barring the hopelessly eccentric, all citizens are content to have the government carry their mail. Although a citizen may be unalterably opposed to government ownership of railroads, he has no objection to the assumption by his government of the responsibility for his security when he travels on them. The construction of roads to facilitate travel, for business or for pleasure, is willingly entrusted to the government for the sake of greater efficiency and economy. To be sure, in the case of the promotion of some ends he has reservations, or may even flatly object to corporate administration. In the United States many citizens are strongly opposed to federal participation in education though they fervently believe in corporate promotion by the state. In his religious life, however, he demands complete independence; even a gesture in the direction of government participation is considered a threat against his spiritual freedom.

As in the case of independent ends, the disposition to cooperation is not constant but is altered by circumstances. In a period of great floods, the demand for government flood control is very strong. Often the belief in corporate responsibility is simply a reflection of a temporary need for help. It is at least questionable if nationalization of industry in Great Britain after World War II would have been carried so far except under the pressure of the post-war emergencies. The attitude of the citizens to this problem is also influenced by changes in political philosophy. An extreme example from outside the area of democratic government is the case of the dramatic development of the National Socialist ideology in Germany just before the Second World War. Under the influence of the hysterical extremism of this philosophy, a large part of the German people, to some extent conditioned by national misfortune and humiliation, willingly assigned to the government nearly absolute authority over body and soul. In the United States, the advent of the philosophy of the New Deal ushered in a decided change in the attitude of many people to government participation in their private lives.

The corporate promotion of private ends which, initially

or because of special circumstances, are "predisposed" to co-operation is a comparatively simple task. In the area of government, this is the realm in which democracy works most smoothly. The area in which it works least smoothly is that of the third class of private ends, those, namely, which are "naturally" competitive and thus produce disagreement and conflict. The desire for wealth is one example. It is a natural source of conflict. There is, to begin with, not enough wealth in the world to satisfy all desires for it, and thus the actual accumulation of it involves sharp and lasting competition. Secondly, the desire for it has a tendency to develop into a craving which in some cases seems insatiable. The pursuit of wealth is inclined to arouse strong feelings, such as greed, envy, and other anti-social emotions. As a consequence, the pursuit of wealth is carried on in an atmosphere unfavorable to co-operation, both between individuals and institutions. What is true of wealth is even more true of power. To gain power over one's fellows means usually to deprive them of much more than wealth: it involves depriving them of their self-respect, their spiritual independence, and their moral dignity. It is consequently much more deeply and lastingly resented than the loss of property. The lust for power will not be persuaded and there is no answer to it except force. Of all human ends, the lust for power has probably been the greatest threat to peace and security in the history of mankind.

The strength of these dangerous passions, as of all passions, varies greatly within individuals and, in consequence, with institutions. In the case of one man, the desire for wealth is a mild interest; in his neighbor it is an insatiable lust. One man will make a desperate sacrifice for the sake of accumulating power; another will peacefully endure serious delimitation of it. The pursuit of an end in the case of one individual is a calm and cold-blooded affair; in another, it involves violent emotional disturbances. Success and failure in realization are accompanied by different emotional temperatures. An institution organized for the purpose of accumulating economic wealth or power is likely to have more emotional drive, to be more jealous of its rights, more sensitive to limitation, and consequently more antagonistic to rivals than an institution devoted to the pursuit of learning. However, even institutions devoted to the pursuit of spiritual salvation or the establishment of universal peace frequently develop and publicly manifest the same emotional tendencies. Variations in emotional personality thus seriously affect the incidence and degree of conflict between individuals and institutions in the struggle for realization.

The strength of these passions also varies with the external circumstances in which they operate. When men are in trouble and need help, they are off their guard and are easily induced to resign some of their rights. When a nation is disorganized, the promise of what is so sadly needed, namely, strength, definiteness, and leadership, may influence the grant of unusual authority to a popular figure. A weak country is ready to listen to a strong voice. Confusion, uncertainty, and distress give the demagogue his opportunity. Tyranny of persons or ideas is easily established amid chaos. "It is when a people loses its self-confidence that it surrenders its soul to a dictator or oligarchy. In Walter Lippmann's tremendous metaphor, it welcomes manacles to prevent its hands shaking."*

In the realm of these naturally competitive and conflicting ends the institution must of necessity participate in the solution of conflicts. Such participation is a part of the "corporate" end. The establishment of the institution of democratic government represents the most extensive and continuous effort of men to overcome some difficulties in the realization of their ends. It is man's most ambitious public effort at the institutional integration and organization of his life. As such it is but an extension of the non-political institution which has the same purpose, though in a more limited way, namely, to attain a common goal by means of orderly and efficient cooperation. In the last analysis, it is a social projection of the individual's private attempts to bring order into his life by striking a balance among the diverse and competing demands of his personality. In the government, private ends are pooled in the corporate end in order to attain a greater quantity and better quality of realization than would

---

*John Buchan. *Pilgrim's Way*, p. 291.

otherwise be possible. The democratic way of accomplishing this is the essence of democracy as process. As we shall see, it is, in the last analysis, nothing more than the way in which reasonable and friendly men long ago learned to settle their private differences.

*FOUR*

## Development of Conflicts

ALTHOUGH IT IS THE CORPORATE END OF A DEMOCRATIC government to be hospitable to as many ends of the citizens as possible, it does not guarantee the complete or even partial satisfaction of any particular need, desire, or interest. Since some private ends are competitive and consequently conflicting, this is not possible. On the contrary, the commitment of the government to the corporate end makes it a foregone conclusion that the promotion of some private ends will need to be limited. For example, the power of some citizen or of some group of citizens will have to be curtailed in order that some other citizens may have some degree of independence. Such limitation is thus not an end in itself. In the case of the government, as in the case of the private personality and the institution, the negative function of limitation is executed in the service of the positive function, namely the greatest possible realization of all the ends of all the citizens. Limitation of private ends is in the service of the corporate end.

The necessity of limitation follows from the nature of an institution. Men organize in order to promote common ends. The corporate end is not the end of one member but of all the members. When an individual joins an organization in order to realize a private end, he entrusts the promotion of that end to the institution. He may do this because he thinks that the chance or degree of realization will be improved by such assignment, or because it will leave him free privately to promote other ends. The important point is that the other members have done the same thing. In each case there has been a transfer of responsibility for the promotion of the common end to the institution, that is to say, to the members as a group. Since many can do more than one, the group or institution is able to devise new ways of promotion. The transfer therefore represents a distinct gain. But it also represents a loss: the individual is now no longer in personal control of the promotion of his ends but must share this control with his fellow members. Limitations are thus set on his behavior. In a large group, this control may even be assigned to representatives, in which case it is removed one step farther from private control.

Membership in a group has another consequence: it means that the individual has assumed certain responsibilities. He must conform to its rules and regulations. He must obey its officers because he has assigned certain powers to them. He has given up the right to make his own decisions and has assumed the duty of accepting those of the group. There is a third consequence: he will be held at least nominally responsible for the decisions and actions of the group, even for those to which he may be opposed. He has the privilege of criticizing his fellow members, his officers, and his representatives. He has the right to condemn them, to penalize them, and to vote for their removal. But he cannot escape his share of the responsibility as a member.

There are, to be sure, a great variety of institutions, differing in size and in purpose. In general, it can be said that the larger the membership, the more complex the organization. The more members there are, the less power does the individual member have. The larger the organization, the farther the individual member is removed from the center of administration and control. Although his power and responsibility, quantitatively considered, may be very small, he is not relieved from personal moral responsibility. When the purposes or acts of an organization are praised or condemned, the individual member shares this praise or condemnation.

This assignment of personal moral responsibility is felt to be justified because the individual has chosen to be a member of the organization. He shares praise or blame by virtue of voluntary association.

The means employed by the organization are not always exclusively positive. Men sometimes organize for protection. In an unfriendly environment, this may be necessary to assure physical security. In American frontier society vigilantes assumed the duties of the police and of the courts. Even in a highly civilized society, men may organize to escape from confusion and disorder in some area of life. A business may become so competitive that the participants are driven to organize for the purpose of self-regulation.

Institutions are established for the protection of the weak as well as for the aggrandizement of the strong. They may reflect the selfishness or unselfishness of the members. The motives may be economic, religious, educational, social, or aesthetic. The consequences may be good or bad. Whatever the purposes or the consequences, membership in an institution involves for the individual an exchange of something gained for something lost. It thus involves a *moral choice:* the acceptance of a responsibility in return for the enjoyment of a benefit. A privilege is gained and a duty is assumed. A limitation of freedom is accepted in exchange for a greater satisfaction of some need, desire, or interest.

\* \* \*

What has been said about institutions in general is equally true of the particular institution of democratic government. To be sure, the scope of government is more inclusive. It not only places limitations on the behavior of individuals as individuals but also on the behavior of the institutions within its jurisdiction. This limitation affects a very wide range of interests. In consequence, the benefits which accrue are correspondingly varied. The number and character and interrelations of duties and privileges which are the consequences of the absorption of private ends in the corporate end of the government make this the most complex of human institutions. The limitations on private behavior are the necessary consequences of the assignment of power to the government, both

## Development of Conflicts

as originally determined in the constitution and as subsequently determined by changes made by the citizens. The degree to which such limitations are necessary depends, as has been previously indicated, upon all the factors involved in a corporate effort to satisfy private needs, desires, and interests, namely, on their character and strength, their interrelations, and the external circumstances in which they occur.

The limitations on private behavior which result from the government's efforts to create a favorable physical environment for the realization of private and group ends are seldom found irksome. The benefits are not only important and obvious, but they are also large in comparison to the degree of curtailment of private liberties. At least in the case of the overwhelming majority of the citizens, the benefits greatly outweigh the costs. To be sure, sometimes, as for example in the case of the appropriation by the government of private property, the citizen feels that he has been deprived of one of his most fundamental "rights." The unreasonable may take this attitude even when government "interference" is justified by the threat of public danger, as in the case of flood control. In general, the character of the reactions of the citizen to government activity will be determined by the extent to which he considers his liberty of action to have been affected. Nothing could be more natural than this.

When responsibility for the promotion of common ends has been assigned to the government for the sake of greater efficiency, the consequent necessary limitation of private action is likely to be accepted without protest. The citizen's tolerance of such limitation will be the greater if he is aware of his own lack of knowledge and skill, as in the case of the protection of his health, or if his interest in the end is only occasional, as in the postal service. Sometimes the corporate activity is so remote from his daily life or the effect of it upon his life is so indirect that it has little if any reality for him. His personal interest in the particular kind of activity involved is also a determining factor. Thus we find that individuals and groups with special interests, say in vivisection or oleomargarine or sex education, strongly advocate, or strongly oppose, government participation in the promotion of these interests.

The last example suggests the area in which the problem of limitation becomes a very serious one, that, namely, in which the interests of individuals and groups are competitive and consequently tend to be conflicting. The most difficult problems of government necessarily arise in this area. Because of the existence of conflicts among private individuals and institutions which the parties in conflict cannot settle without disturbing the public peace and endangering the public welfare, power and authority to prevent and to resolve conflicts are voluntarily assigned by the citizens of a democracy to the government. The underlying reason for this is the fact that conflicts arise out of private interference with the realization of private ends. Since the end of a democratic form of government is the greatest possible realization of all the ends of all the citizens, it is the responsibility of the government to prevent or correct conditions which interfere with such realization. It is obvious, therefore, that this function of government involves the most extensive and serious limitation of the freedom of action of individuals and institutions.

\* \* \*

Before considering the principles and methods of administration of this function in a democracy, it will be useful to inquire into the nature of these conflicts. To begin with, a distinction must be made between conflict and difference of opinion or belief. Differences of opinion are potential sources but not unavoidable causes of conflict. A conflict arises when there is interference with the realization of an end or the threat of it. Such interference is by no means inevitable. Individuals, and likewise institutions, can be in complete disagreement on fundamental issues without in the slightest degree interfering with one another. A variety of religious denominations and educational institutions exist side by side and peacefully pursue their respective ends. Conflict in the sense in which the term is here used results only when an individual or an institution makes an overt effort to limit another individual or institution in the free pursuit of private ends; when, as the traditional phrase has it, "rights" are interfered with. Respect for these "rights" may be specifically guaranteed by law, or the citizen may consider them to be his by default, custom, or social inheritance. In so far as the occurrence of subsequent conflict is concerned, the important fact is that he considers them to be his rights and insists on making an issue of any interference with them.

Since conflicts are a by-product of the efforts of human beings to attain their ends, they occur in every area of human life. Whenever ends are related they are likely to come in conflict and thus require limitation. Conflicts occur within the individual, between individuals and institutions, and between institutions. Conflicts within the individual are the result of interference and competition of needs, desires, and interests with one another within the private personality. Since the solution is purely a matter of private adjustment, the principle or rule which is invoked need have authority only for the individual. When the ends of two private individuals conflict, a voluntary settlement requires the application of a rule or principle which is mutually acceptable. When the conflicting parties cannot agree on such a principle, each of them may use other means to accomplish his ends, for example, trickery or even force, or they may voluntarily submit the dispute to a third party, or be compelled to do so. Certain it is that innumerable conflicts between private individuals are settled privately.

If the ends of an individual come in conflict with those of a private organization or institution of which he is a member, he can follow one of several courses of action: he can recognize the authority of the institution and submit to it; he can resign his membership; he can fight for internal change; or, if he thinks his larger rights are being denied, he can appeal to an authority which is charged with the responsibility for protecting these rights, the courts, for example. When the ends of private institutions conflict, these institutions are in the same position as private individuals: they must settle their dispute privately or it must be settled, with or without the consent of the conflicting parties, by an outside authority, or they must learn to live with their differences.

\* \* \*

We are here concerned only with political conflicts, that is to say, conflicts between private individuals and institutions on the one hand, and the government of the state on the other. The basic issue in these conflicts is the right of the state to impose limitations on the freedom of individuals and institutions to realize their private ends. There are, first of all, conflicts between private individuals, between private institutions, and between individuals and institutions over respective rights, the nature and limitations of which are defined in the law. The government is brought into the picture only on two conditions: (1) there is an alleged violation by either party of rights of action as defined by the law, "the law" being obviously responsible for the correction of this violation; (2) the conflict is in an area in which the respective rights are not defined but in which the conflict endangers the public welfare, "the law" having the right to interfere on the principle that the government is responsible for the public peace.

The area of potential conflict is so extensive and the kinds of conflict so varied that even a large number of examples would hardly be representative. Examples illustrating two basically different types of conflict may, however, be useful. Conflicts are either over ends or over the means by which these ends are to be realized. In the case of some ends, even the attempt to realize them is forbidden. No man is permitted to satisfy a desire to kill or to injure another person or to deprive him of his liberty merely because he wishes to do this. He is, however, permitted to do these things when they are the only means for realizing another end, namely, self-defense. A private individual has the general right of adding to his possessions. He may not do this by theft but only by legitimate means such as purchase; that is, by means authorized by law.

The parties in a conflict between the individual and the state either voluntarily or under compulsion submit their differences to the court for adjudication. The action may be initiated either by the private individual or by an official of the government appointed or elected for this purpose. The court has the authority to pass judgment because it is a branch of the government and because this right has been originally assigned to the government. There is a characteristically democratic balance of rights and duties here. The citizen has the privilege of reference of conflict to the court and the right to its assistance. He also has the duty to obey. The court has the right to pass judgment and to compel obedience, but it also has the duty of exercising these rights in accordance with prescribed principles and with "due process." The existence of courts thus obviates the need for private action in the pursuance of ends but, by the same token, limits the freedom of action of the individual.

The area of jurisdiction and the conditions under which this jurisdiction is to be exercised are more or less specifically defined. The rights of the court in the last analysis represent a transfer by the citizens of private "rights" to the state, the purpose being the assurance to the citizens of the best possible opportunity for the realization of private ends. The issue in this type of conflict therefore is not whether the court does or does not have the right to command or forbid but whether the specific occasion does or does not warrant this. The conditions for judicial action and the manner and extent of this action are prescribed in "the law," at least in principle. Although the principles to be applied seem clear enough, the concrete application of them presents great difficulties.

Both principles and procedures may themselves be objects of dispute. After a verdict is rendered, the litigant may feel that the court has not properly executed its task, either because it has not correctly applied the relevant principles or because it has not followed the proper procedure. In such cases he exercises the right of appeal to a higher court and, if this right is granted, obtains a review of his case. Courts of appeal have been established to assure that the lower courts shall properly perform their function in the corporate encouragement or limitation of the realization of private ends. The right of appeal to such courts has been reserved by the citizens for the same reason.

In a second type of conflict the private individual or private institution challenges the right of the government to participate in the promotion of the realization of certain private ends. Such participation usually, if not always, involves the encouragement of one group of citizens and the limitation of another in the pursuit of their ends. In this type of conflict the citizen does not contest the interpretation of a law but the "legality" of the law itself. The laws passed by the Congress of the United States during the depression of the nineteen thirties, in execution of the New Deal policies, aroused representatives of business and industry on numerous occasions to challenge the authority of the government to regulate the conduct of private enterprise.

In the American democracy such a conflict may also develop between the Federal government and the government of smaller political units which are included in it. In state constitutions certain rights are reserved to counties and cities within their jurisdiction and in the Federal Constitution certain rights are reserved to the states. There may be a real or fancied encroachment by one unit on the rights of another, in which case the complaining party has the right and opportunity to appeal to the court which has jurisdiction. A logical consequence of this retention of governmental rights by the smaller units is the right of the citizen on occasion to challenge the authority of such a unit. Thus the legal right of the citizen to contest the right of the state to pursue some specific policy in the administration of education is a logical consequence of the possession by the state of the authority to administer education.

Whoever the parties to the above conflicts may be, the formal appeal is still to an agency of the government. Final appeal in the United States of America is to the United States Supreme Court; in some democracies, for example, in Great Britain, there is no Supreme Court and the final appeal is to the supreme lawmaking body itself. The principle implied in the United States practice is that the lawmaking power is not absolute but is limited by the basic law of the land. In the United States, the federal government itself is subject to the Constitution of the United States. This responsibility of the government follows from the fact that in a democracy the constitution represents the initial assignment of power by the citizens to the government. The constitution defines, in the form of more or less general principles, the corporate functions of the government which have been assigned to it by the citizens in order that their private ends may have the most favorable opportunity of realization possible.

This interpretation of the origin of the authority of the basic law implies that the citizens are the original political source of its authority. The basic law is an expression of their corporate judgment and will. They are its source and, logically, they therefore continue to be the source. It is a democratic doctrine that, since the citizens "made" the Constitution, they have the right to change it. The citizens, individually or collectively, do not have the right to ignore it or to disobey it, but they do have the right to initiate attempts to revise it. This is not the case, for example, in totalitarian political institutions in which the source of authority is external to those who are subject to it. In such a form of government, the individual does not even have the "constitutional" right to question or to challenge it. His duties are absolute compulsions and his privileges outright gifts. He may request that his rights be recognized, but he may not demand this. The source which granted the right may also deprive him of it. The attitude must be that of Job: "The Lord has given and the Lord has taken away. Blessed be the name of the Lord."

In a democracy, even the authority of the court of last appeal is not absolute in this sense. If the citizen is not satisfied with its decision, he may appeal to public opinion and initiate a political move to change the basic law. In such a case, either political pressure is put upon the representatives of the citizens in the lawmaking bodies, or an effort is made at the next opportunity to elect replacements who are pledged to the cause. An election to determine a change in constitution thus represents a third type of conflict. In this type of conflict the government itself is officially not a party. It is a conflict among the citizens to determine whether or not the power of the government should be extended, or limited, or left as it is. The question which the citizens must ask themselves, conceived in terms of the realization of private ends, is this: Shall we make a change in the power and opportunities of the government to participate in the promotion of our ends?

The various ways in which this question can be stated

are expressive of the nature of the conflict involved. One party will ask: Shall we increase the opportunity of the government to interfere in our private affairs? Shall we proceed even farther along the road to socialism? Shall we destroy private initiative and private responsibility? Shall we increase the dictatorial power of the federal government? The opposition, on its part, will ask equally leading questions: Shall we extend the power of the government over predatory private interests? Shall we assert our common ownership of natural resources by putting their development and administration in the hands of the government? Shall we authorize the government to extend to us those benefits to which citizens of a democracy are entitled? Why not shift to the government responsibilities which are too much for private citizens to bear?

The prohibition amendment and its repeal, New Deal legislation regulative of banking and business, social security legislation such as unemployment compensation and old age insurance, labor legislation, and federal support of education are some examples of conflicts in which the transfer of responsibility for the promotion of private ends is involved. This is usually an issue in national elections, for it is on such questions that the great political parties now seem to differ. The voters vote on leaders who have taken or seem to have taken a stand on legislation in which such questions are involved. Sometimes the revelation by candidates of a general attitude of friendliness or unfriendliness to concentration of power or to private enterprise is sufficient to determine the vote of the citizen.

There is a special variety of this type of conflict which, though fortunately of infrequent occurrence, is vital in nature and often dramatic in its consequences. The conflict is in the last analysis the consequence of the recognition by the private citizen or institution of an authority superior to that of the government. The authority of the government over another source of authority is challenged. A good example is the conscientious objector who defies the right of the government to compel him to bear arms in the defense of his country, although the law prescribes this to be a duty of the citizen. The appeal may be to the alleged superior authority of a religious institution or a religious faith. In some cases the "moral law" is cited as the justification for resistance. Occasionally those who take this position make an attempt to organize a political move to change the constitution and thus to transform this type of conflict into the preceding type; but the fact that they constitute a very small and consequently powerless minority makes such attempts impractical. Since the law in such cases is usually perfectly clear on the question of jurisdiction, the refusal to recognize it constitutes civil disobedience. The government has no choice but to ignore or to punish, neither of which alternatives constitutes a solution of the conflict.

* * *

All political conflicts are concerned with the determination of the scope or "coverage" of the corporate end. In such conflicts the citizens are brought face to face with the necessity and duty of deciding in a particular situation exactly what they mean when they assert that it is the function of government to promote the greatest possible realization of all the ends of all the citizens. These conflicts require decisions with respect to the specific application of the general principles of democracy. It should be noted, however, that they are not concerned with the question as to who is to decide the issue or as to the procedure to be used. They do not involve a difference of opinion concerning the democratic process. No one of the conflicting parties is proposing to abolish the right of the citizens to raise such issues and to vote on them.

These conflicts and their settlement are also concrete manifestations of the second essential characteristic of democracy discussed in Chapter II, namely, the capacity for peaceful and orderly self-correction. Changes in the means by which the corporate end is to be realized can be effected by prescribed democratic processes. A weakness or an oversight in the constitution can be remedied by the passage of an amendment. A mistake can be corrected by the repeal of an amendment. Costly lessons learned in times of crisis can be recorded for posterity in legislation. If times have changed and laws are outmoded, practical adjustments can be made. The development of the highly organized society of today out of the comparatively simple and unorganized frontier communities has been accompanied by changes in government participation in the promotion of private ends which were intended to be accommodations to this development. The depletion of natural resources has been accompanied by increasing governmental control of their use. What seemed to be dangerous concentration of economic power in huge banking and manufacturing combinations resulted in the passage of laws designed to distribute this power and to prevent such concentration in the future. In times of war, peacetime privileges have been abrogated, and restrictions, quite undemocratic in nature, placed on liberties, only to be promptly removed when peace was restored. On the necessity and propriety and legality of these changes there were sharp differences of opinion. Their accomplishment was often attended by bitter political conflict. The regular peaceful and orderly solution of such conflicts demonstrates the political efficiency of the democratic process in the direction and control of human relations.

*FIVE*

## Settlement of Conflicts

PERMANENT PROVISION FOR THE ORDERLY AND PEACEFUL SETTLEment of conflicts implies the existence of some measure of agreement on principles and procedures to be followed in such solution. In an autocracy, both are likely to be determined, often arbitrarily, by the will of the tyrant or absolute monarch or ruling clique. Decision and execution are thus comparatively simple matters. In a democracy, where the decision is in the hands of the citizens, the principles are bound to be complex and the procedures cumbersome. The procedures to be followed in the political settlement of conflicts, though cumbersome, are perfectly clear. Election machinery, the parliamentary processes of representative bodies, the principle of majority rule, these are reasonably easy to understand. Disagreements with respect to "mechanical" details, though not uncommon, are usually of minor importance. Exceptions in the United States are the perennial discussion of the faults and virtues of the electoral college, of the bicameral legislature, and of reapportionment proposals.

Though the mechanics of democracy are simple and easy to understand, the guiding principles and their application are not. This is due, in the first place, to the great number of human needs, desires, and interests involved. It is one of the demands of democracy that as many ends of the citizens as possible shall be realized. A second difficulty with which democracy is faced is the complexity of the personalities of the individual citizens and of their organizations. Among the citizens there are a great variety of combinations of needs, desires, and interests. Moreover, human beings change with greater or lesser degrees of permanence. Finally, there is the further complication of change in the physical environment in which this grand complex of ends is to be realized. Conceived in these terms, the effective settlement of conflicts in a democracy does indeed seem impossible.

There are other and more favorable factors, however, which must be taken into consideration. The setting in which the democratic process is expected to work is not a socially primitive one. Human relations do not originate with the formation of the state; neither do conflicts and their settlement. Previous to the attainment of political maturity, the citizen has had practical training in human relations and in social adjustment; in the family, the school, the church, and society at large. The democratic state includes within its boundaries a large number and variety of institutions, most of which are in one respect or another good training schools for the practice of democracy on the political level.

Viewed from the standpoint of ethics, the prospective citizen is not a moral infant. To be sure, he is also not a moral expert. The great mass of the citizens are neither moral experts nor moral ignoramuses but ordinary people who have had some education in moral principles and some training in their application. The prospective citizen has had many occasions to make moral decisions and thus to reflect on moral principles. By the time he becomes a citizen, he will at the least have developed some degree of moral responsibility. At best, he will be an integrated moral personality. He will at all events have had some experience with human conflicts and their solution.

A second fact to be taken into consideration is that the area of conflict in which government and politics are involved is not nearly as extensive as it at first view appears to be. Countless conflicts between citizens and non-political institutions are and remain purely private. Many are small in scope and have no social, and certainly no political, repercussions. Even institutions frequently settle their differences privately. For example, only rarely is the state involved in conflicts between religious institutions. It is in the spirit of democracy to let men settle their private differences without government interference, if this is at all practical and safe.

The seriousness of the problem of conflicts is further reduced by the fact that even in the case of conflicts which develop in the political arena, many are superficial. Some are not even genuine. Sometimes the issues have been trumped up and are kept alive by politicians for selfish or partisan political reasons. Sometimes private issues are forcibly brought into the arena of political conflict though they do not belong there. Those who originally induced the conflicts would regret it very much if they were to be solved. Since the issues are spurious, or unimportant, or politically irrelevant, the conflicts soon wear themselves out and the good sense of the citizens prevails.

It would be a mistake, however, to dismiss these conflicts as of no importance in the democratic state. Though the issues are spurious, artificial, or temporary, the occurrence of the conflicts is a fact of considerable significance. Conflicts, no matter what the issues, always arouse emotional antagonisms and therefore create an unfavorable environment for the operation of democratic processes. It is well to recall in this connection that basic conflicts leave lasting social scars, in the form of resentment, suspicion, desire for revenge, and other antagonistic attitudes. These attitudes subsequently become obstacles to the settlement of future differences. Sometimes such attitudes take root and develop a vitality which only time can exhaust. Because of the demoralizing effect of these attitudes, there is nothing quite so reprehensible in a democracy as the willful incitement of unnecessary conflict.

\* \* \*

In any society, political or otherwise, both the kind of settlements aimed at and the processes to be followed in the attainment of such settlement are determined by the ideals of that society. It is the special ideal of democracy to promote the greatest possible realization of all the ends of all the citizens. The primary importance of the individual is therefore a basic implication. The individual must be assured of the greatest possible opportunity for realization, *but in a community of other individuals.* This is the full meaning of the favorite democratic doctrine of the moral dignity of the individual. The selfhood of the individual is, to be sure, the first datum, but it is a selfhood conceived in relation to the selfhood of other individuals. The term 'moral dignity' implies respect for the moral personality of others. It follows that this moral dignity must also be acknowledged and respected by the state. The assignment to government of the promotion of the greatest possible realization of private ends is the political affirmation of the principle of the moral dignity of the individual.

For the believer in democracy, this conception of the end of the state is not a blind or willful choice. On the contrary, he considers it to be a choice dictated by nature and experience. It is an obvious fact that human beings differ very much from one another and that, in spite of considerable uniformity of education, these differences reappear in every new generation. The forcible attempts to eliminate these differences which are recorded in history have always been followed by a resurgence of differences. The proponent of democracy does not believe that these differences can be eliminated. Even temporary suppression requires force and force is a dangerous instrument to use in the control of human relationships.

The proponent of democracy not only considers variety to be "natural" but also desirable. The protection of variety makes it possible for each individual to realize his own particular potentialities and thus to develop his own personality. The suppression of differences results in frustration and in unhappiness. It literally denies the individual the opportunity to be himself. Variety is also an essential source of social progress. Genius is a case in point, though an extreme one. Variety is a condition for self-expression and thus for invention and discovery. This is as true for racial diversity as for individual diversity. Cultural diversity produces the essential materials for social progress. Variety provides opportunity for comparison and evaluation and choice. If all the interests of human beings were alike, there would be no possibility of *choice*.

In a society in which variety is suppressed as much as possible, life would tend to become mere repetition. There would no doubt be some advance in favored areas; but progress of society as a complex of human interests and activities would inevitably reach, and expire at, a dead level. Such unity as would be attained would be the mechanical unity of standardization, not the dynamic unity of a developing society. Considered in the framework of the history of social groups and institutions, it would be a reversion to a lower stage in social evolution. Ant colonies and bee hives reveal a degree of organization and efficiency that far exceeds that attained in human societies. But this kind of society is hardly an object of envy, for it is adapted to the nature and interests of ants and bees, not to those of human beings. Machines have an even greater efficiency. What normal human beings want and what they need is a type of social organization which will have as much variety as the complexity of human relationships will permit.

To be sure, this involves a certain degree of standardization. But this standardization is not an end in itself: it is a means to an end, namely, to the greatest possible self-realization of all the members of society. According to believers in democracy, to make standardization an ideal is a perverse aim of totalitarianism. Standardization is not a doctrine of the future but a memory of the past. The claim that the encouragement of the greatest possible amount of variety means eventual social chaos is not accepted by the proponent of democracy. The social goal of the democratic form of government is the happy medium between chaos, which is absence of all control, and tyranny, which is the maximum of control. From this point of view, democracy may be defined as *the continuous effort of the citizens through the medium of government to maintain society in a state of limited equilibrium between the extremes of chaos and tyranny*. It is not assumed that the equilibrium can be perfect and that society can ever reach a stable and permanent state of standardization. On the contrary, this is not only assumed to be impossible but also undesirable. Society must of necessity be changing and therefore there must be constant adjustment, that is, self-correction.

The effort to make this adjustment creates conflict. Conflict is therefore not an out and out evil; it is a potential instrument of progress. However, it is the latter only when some degree of social adjustment is effected. The peaceful and orderly settlement of conflicts in the democratic way is a form of effecting social progress with a minimum of social loss and at a minimum expense in human adaptation.

\* \* \*

What principles or formulae are to be employed in the settlement of conflicts? Before determining the answer to this question, it is necessary to consider the implications of the terms in which the question is stated. The terms 'principle,' 'formula,' and 'settlement' have an implication of finality, whereas the term 'social conflict' implies that some degree of social change is continuous. To speak of the settlement of a conflict is to imply that the cause of the conflict has been removed once and for all. This implication is not factually justified. Conflict is itself part of the social process and must therefore continue to be so. Settlement in this sense has no implication of finality.

The term 'formula' seems acceptable since it implies application to, or use in, a process. It has, however, the deceptive implication of exactness. A formula makes one think of a mathematical equation to which one can turn for an exact answer in a specific situation. Unfortunately, mathematics is of little use in the discovery or application of 'formulae' in the solution of human conflicts. Needs, desires, and interests are not identifiable chemical elements or measurable forces. The term 'principles,' though certainly not suggestive of mathematical exactness, nevertheless gives the impression of absoluteness and universal applicability.

An analysis of the concrete nature of social conflict will indicate more acceptable meanings of these terms. To begin with, social conflicts are conflicts between men, not between ideas. Only men have needs, desires, and interests, and only men desire to realize ends. Ideas do not quarrel; do not, in a literal sense, go to court; do not bear resentment. Ideas do not vote. They do not possess property or covet the property of others. They do not lie, steal, conspire, organize, strike. Ideas are used by people but they are not themselves people. Ideas do not even control their own meanings: these are assigned to them by people. This is the reason why people develop a sense of property even about ideas. People therefore quarrel about ideas. But, literally speaking, one man cannot sue another over the possession of an idea.

Moreover, in the case of conflicts between ideas as such, a solution can be left unsolved without any practical consequences. Before ideas can have any social consequences, they must be transformed into action, if only into speech or writing. The ideas must act through some person or institution. In that case they are no longer merely ideas but forms of social contact. They become involved in all the complexities, variations, and inconsistencies of persons. They become manifestations of the needs, desires, and interests of persons and they become instruments employed in the realization of ends. They are transformed into institutions and become embodied in them.

It is true that, when a conflict is settled, the solution may be recorded in terms of ideas, or, as we say, principles. Constitutions and laws are forms of such recordation. The purpose is to perpetuate the principle of the solution so that it can be applied in future conflicts over the same issue or over issues of the same type. It is in this way that society remembers the lessons it has learned by experience. However, the terms of the particular conflict are not recorded—only the principle represented in the solution. The principle is abstracted from the concrete situation in which it functioned as a specific application. In consequence, the solution is again transformed into general ideas. This reduces the concrete significance of the principle and therefore its practical efficiency. Moreover, in time principles recorded in formal documents such as declarations of rights, constitutions, and laws acquire great authority. Some even come to be looked upon as revelations. Some acquire an authority like that of gods, or, as the philosophers say, of absolutes.

Viewed from the standpoint of principles, the problem of the settlement of conflicts can be stated in this way: are there to be found clearly conceived, accurately formulated, and consistently applicable principles which men can use as rules for the solution of their conflicts? In the case of democracy, are there available to the citizens basic principles to which democracy is committed and to which the citizens can appeal in their conflicts over the means of realization of their ends? If so, where are they recorded, say, in the case of United States of America?

Several different affirmative answers have been given to this question. The source most commonly cited is the Constitution of the United States, particularly the Preamble. The Preamble, however, is obviously very general. It defines the purposes of government as follows: (1) to form a more perfect union, (2) to insure domestic tranquility, (3) to provide for the common defense, (4) to promote the general welfare, (5) to secure the blessings of liberty for ourselves and our posterity. To be sure, these statements are intended to be merely general identifications of the purposes of government, it being implied that the Constitution will prescribe the specific ways in which these purposes are to be accomplished. But this only underscores the fact that they are the guiding ideas of the Constitution. When the interpretation or the amendment of the Constitution is an issue, the meaning of these guiding principles itself becomes an issue. Considered by themselves, the first four are so general that an absolute monarch might claim them as definitions of his royal purposes. A Communist might, in addition, claim that the fifth is an accurate statement of the ideal of the present Communist regime in Russia. The fifth purpose, particularly, is stated in such general terms that it offers little practical guidance to the citizen of a democracy. What blessings of liberty are referred to? How much liberty is to be secured? When is a consequence of liberty a blessing and when is it a curse?

To answer such questions, it is suggested that we must go a little farther back in the history of our government, namely, to the Declaration of Independence and its "self-evident truths." These truths are "that all men are created equal, that they are endowed by their Creator with certain inalienable rights, that among these are life, liberty, and the pursuit of happiness." But whose conception of liberty and happiness? Obviously, those of the citizens. Unfortunately, it is precisely between the citizens that the disagreements occur. Numberless conflicts between the citizens of a democracy are concerned with the constituents and requisites of happiness, or with the degree and extent of happiness. The inquirer is also left without specific instruction with respect to the amount or extent of liberty. As for the term 'equality,' it is relevant to note here that several different interpretations have come to be accepted. Equal, say some, means equality of opportunity. Others say that the reference is to equality before the law. Still a third group insists that the reference is to the moral dignity of the individual and is intended to prescribe respect for individual personality.

A traditional point of view is that the basic guiding idea in the Declaration is that of 'inalienable rights.' This doctrine requires some clarification. In one well established sense, the term 'right' means something conferred. Thus the citizen may not be deprived of his right to vote without due cause because this right is conferred on him by the Constitution. The driver of an automobile has the 'right of way' under certain circumstances because the law has prescribed this. Generally speaking, the rights of a citizen in a democracy are those assured by the Constitution and its interpretations. The assumption that the inalienable rights referred to in the Declaration are merely anticipations of the rights actually assured in the Constitution is, however, unacceptable to those who hold another old and well-established view of natural rights. According to this view, the reference of the term is not forward to the Constitution but backward to some more basic source of rights.

There is, however, no agreement on the more basic source. The traditional Christian view is that God, the "Creator" of the Declaration, conferred certain rights on man. Man is entitled to the rights guaranteed by the Constitution because they were originally conferred upon man by God. No power, secular or religious, has the right to deprive him of these rights. They are *inalienable* rights because the authority of God is superior to that of any other human institution.

But here too we encounter a serious difficulty, namely,

the historic disagreements among Christian sects on the subject of the interpretations of the Scriptures. Christians hold irreconcilable views of long standing concerning the right of interpretation, the seat of final authority in interpretation, and the extent of this authority. In the case of a democracy, we are therefore back again in the area of potential conflict among the citizens. There is, finally, the objection that in a democracy there must be room for citizens who accept other revelations than the Christian or who do not accept any revelation at all. For these citizens, reference to the Scriptures for the identification of natural rights would be irrelevant if not objectionable.

A second school of thought, although committed to the doctrine of inalienable rights, does not accept the divine origin of these rights. The contention is that these rights are "natural" in origin. Unfortunately for the inquirer, there is no agreement on the exact meaning of the term 'natural.' It is sufficient here to note that, whatever difference there may be in the conception of 'natural,' there is agreement that the origin of these rights is not supernatural. Natural rights are rights supposedly conferred on man by nature, by natural law. Since it is obvious that he can be deprived of them by man and since man also is part of nature, it is difficult to see in what sense we can speak here of "inalienable" rights.

Critics of both the natural and supernatural interpretations of the term point out that the Declaration itself identifies the source of these rights. It declares plainly that "governments derive their just power from the consent of the governed." Thus the original source of the rights of the citizens of the United States is the citizens themselves. They confer rights on themselves, by their own decision, through the means and instrumentality of the government which they establish and control. The particular rights to be secured to the governed are determined by the governed.

Conceived in this sense we cannot find in the basic law either a final definition or an authoritative listing of the rights of the citizens. The principles and concepts in the Declaration are too abstract. Even most of the clauses in the Constitution require interpretation. Since it is the interpretations which are in dispute when conflicts arise, we must look elsewhere for the basic principles which are to be applied in the solution of conflicts.

The moral law is advanced by some as the source of these principles. The term 'law' is used here in a secular but non-legal sense. To take this position is to become at once involved in the great historic disputes concerning the end or purpose of life. One school says that it is happiness; another says it is duty; another, self-development. Secular moralists can offer no source of moral principles except human experience as interpreted by human beings. But this brings us back to our starting-point: the conceptions which human beings have concerning their own ends as determined by their own needs, desires, and interests. In a democracy, it is the citizens who not only determine the general principles but decide on their specific applications. The citizens, in the last analysis, give specific content to the broad general principles of the Declaration and, in a lesser degree, to the clauses of the Constitution. If they do not always do this openly and publicly by passing or repealing laws, they at least do it in fact by the practices which they indulge in or tolerate. And this is the area where conflicts occur and where solutions must be reached.

\* \* \*

We must conclude, then, that the citizens of a democracy are agreed on the principle that it is the function of government to promote self-realization but are by no means agreed in respect to their conceptions of self-realization. In a democracy there must therefore be provision for such differences. For example, there must be room in principle for different theologies and different forms of religious worship and thus for the acceptance of different religious conceptions of the basis of morality. For this reason, the Constitution specifically forbids the making of laws "respecting an establishment of religion or prohibiting the free exercise thereof." But this principle or any other is not absolute. Establishments of religion are not absolutely free, that is, outside the law. Certain religious practices—for example, human sacrifices and polygamy—are definitely not permitted. The practice of religion must be adjusted to other practices and to other laws.

Since these adjustments are not automatic, constant interpretation is necessary; and with respect to such interpretation there will be disagreement and sometimes conflict.

This relativism is thus also characteristic of "the law" and consequently a cause of disagreement and conflict. It is true that many conflicts between citizens are easily settled by application of the law. If a law prescribes certain specific safety measures, it is reasonably easy to determine in a particular case whether or not the law has been violated. To be sure, the more complex the prescriptions of the law, as for example the income tax laws, the more difficult is the application.

But this is a difficulty of a type which might be described as technical. When a law lays down a general principle, however, the difficulty becomes one of interpretation. The more general the principle, the more difficult the business of applying the law to concrete cases. Good examples of this are laws having to do with freedom of speech and freedom of religion. Cases involving these rights often end a long career of litigation in the Supreme Court. Sometimes when a case reaches the Supreme Court, the law itself is on trial, for it is one of the responsibilities of this court to examine a law in the light of the broad principles of the Constitution. The Court may even "go behind" the Constitution, so to speak, and judge the issue before it in the light of broad concepts such as the public welfare and the rights of man. As a result of this kind of litigation, the layman is sometimes shocked to find how indefinite and obscure "the law" is and what extreme differences of legal opinion prevail among even the greatest authorities.

The difficulty of the identification of a general principle and its application to concrete cases is also encountered in the area of economic conflict. It might be expected that a concrete solution would be readily attainable in cases in which the issues at stake and the terms of potential solution are quantitatively measurable, say in dollars and cents. Two examples will serve to illustrate the unreliability of this assumption. In labor disputes the idea of "a living wage" is frequently introduced. What is an acceptable definition of a living wage? It may be suggested that "living" means "adequate." Does this include the price of an automobile? To deny this and to insist that an automobile is a luxury is merely to dodge the issue. What is a luxury? Certainly what the majority of the people in a community at a specific time consider a luxury. The standard of living is a matter of public opinion and therefore a variable. There is no exact definition of it. In a conflict, it is, for all practical purposes, what the conflicting parties insist that it is.

The difficulty of finding a clearly stated principle to be applied in a conflict of opinion is even better illustrated in the case of the doctrine of government ownership. One view is that all economic activity and control should be left to private enterprise and let the chips fall where they may. The complete opposite of this view is that all private ownership should be abolished. The government should own, control, and manage all enterprise.

No believer in the traditional American conception of democracy will accept either of these two extreme positions. He will not commit himself either to the doctrine of total non-participation of the government in the promotion of private ends nor to the doctrine of the assignment of total responsibility for the promotion of these ends to the government. Government is for him a means to an end, namely, *self-realization*. The extent of government participation will therefore depend upon the *need* for such participation, and the extent of this need is to be determined by him and his fellow-citizens.

Where now are the citizens to find a categorical principle to guide them in the determination of this need? The truth is that such a principle is not to be found. In the last analysis it is for the citizens to determine the character and the extent of the need and the nature of the corporate means. This is not a matter of the constant application of a principle in which these terms are categorically defined. There is no quantitative formula which can be mechanically applied in concrete situations. The business of governing is a changing social process, requiring constant adjustment and adaptation. External physical conditions, social conditions, crises and emergencies are affecting influences, and underlying everything *as the primary reality,* there are the needs, desires, and interests of the citizens.

In the examples given above and countless others which compose the complex which we call social life, analysis always leads us back to these basic realities. It cannot be emphasized too much that conflicts are between human beings and not between abstract ideas. Human beings are complex personalities. All the elements of personality enter into the composition of the ends which the individual wishes to realize. Individuals interpret principles in terms of their own needs, desires, and interests. It is because these interpretations differ that conflicts arise.

It may be that a theoretical solution of such conflicts can be reached by an appeal to principles, but such is not the case with a practical settlement. In conflicts of this type a settlement can only be reached by the way of mutual adjustment and conciliation, by the "give and take" process. Solution of conflicts by *compromise* is the democratic way. It is the only way in which the greatest possible corporate promotion of the ends of an individual in a community of individuals can be effected.

## SIX

# The Method of Compromise

THE KIND OF SOCIETY THAT DEMOCRACY PROPOSES TO ESTABLISH and maintain requires that the method of compromise shall be applied in human relations. The soundness of this contention becomes evident if we contrast the method of compromise with alternative methods. There is, first of all, the method of force. The contestants "fight it out" and the more powerful wins. Because of the consequences which follow its application, force is foreign to the spirit and the substance of democracy and is therefore used only as a last resort. The result of the settlement, or better, of the termination of a conflict by force, is dominance, not agreement. Such a settlement proves only who is strong enough to enforce what he thinks is right. It makes the differences greater and more basic and thus perpetuates inequality.

The use of force causes the situation to degenerate emotionally because the socially disruptive feelings are intensified. Force breeds resentment, resentment breeds revenge, and revenge breeds conflict. Settlement or termination by force is the first step towards another and usually more serious conflict. Success feeds the appetite of force and nourishes its confidence. More and more reliance comes to be placed on it, until its use becomes habitual. A political society in which force comes to be substituted for compromise—and liquidation for suffrage—will either have to adopt tyranny or combat it with counter-revolution. Voluntary submission in the face of force, though it avoids the immediate destructive consequences of resistance, actually perpetuates the conflict and postpones its settlement. Whenever a conflict is terminated by the application of force or by the threat of such application, there is a complete denial of someone's right to the realization of an end. The moral dignity of an individual is not only denied but actually violated. It is an offense against human personality.

A conflict can, in a very loose sense of the term, be said to be settled by the withdrawal of one of the potential participants. An individual can, for example, leave the "location" of the particular conflict. This was a fairly simple matter in a frontier society. A laborer who was dissatisfied with his wages or with working conditions could find a better job. Opportunities for work were numerous and greatly different in respect to rewards. Since freedom is proportionate to opportunity, the individual worker was in this sense a free man. But in contemporary society the individual has much less freedom. He cannot escape conditions, and as an individual he is powerless to change them. In an industrial conflict he is helpless. For this reason he organizes with his fellows and forms a union and regains some of his bargaining power. He has not escaped conflict, however, but merely pooled his interests with other individuals. The issue between him and his employer remains and the conflict must still be resolved. Force, voluntary submission, and escape are therefore not acceptable or practical ways of settlement of conflict in a modern democratic society.

Compromise is the sound democratic way because it implies an adjustment of differences acceptable to the parties concerned. It implies the recognition of the existence of mutual interests and the mutual right of the parties to protect and further these interests. It assumes that there is no previously adopted law, in the legal sense, which covers the case and to which both parties are subject. If there is such a law and the law is unacceptable, the issue remains, but the scene of the conflict is shifted either to the courts or to the political arena.

As has been previously pointed out, if a private conflict between two individuals involves a basic social issue, it may eventually develop into a nation-wide political conflict which can only be decided by a vote of all the citizens. If the substance as well as the means of the settlement is democratic, there will be some degree of recognition of all the interests involved and a settlement which represents the most practical adjustment of the conflict between these interests. Acceptance of a compromise does not necessarily imply warm approval of it. A compromise is acceptable simply because it is an attainable, sometimes the only attainable, settlement. A compromise is a realistic, not an idealistic solution. It is the most practically useful kind of solution.

There are good reasons for this. A compromise is the product of a concrete and not of an imaginary or theoretical situation. The settlement is a product of the social forces which produced the conflict. That is why the solution fits the situation. It is a solution which is reached in the concrete setting of the conflict, not one developed in the abstract realm of ideas. Moreover, a compromise is worked out by those who have to live with the settlement, not by an "objective" observer of the conflict or by a professor who needs only to lecture about it. It follows that the solution should also be evaluated in terms of the concrete situation, not merely in terms of abstract principles.

A compromise represents a settlement between men, not between ideas; between the human beings who are actually involved, not between ideas which will neither profit nor lose by the compromise. These beings, moreover, are *real* beings, not the theoretical beings created by some social or political theorist. The latter are usually only parts or phases of actual human beings. They are abstractions; sometimes they are fictions of the imagination. The problems of the "economic man" are much more easily solved than those of a man who is in addition a religious man, an artistic man, a romantic man, a superstitious man, a stubborn man, a foolish man. An agreement is sometimes described as a meeting of minds. A compromise is more than that: it is a meeting of the personalities involved, of complete but complex human beings. It is a meeting of the ideas, feelings and, what is most useful of all, of the *wills* which are in conflict.

Compromises are thus the products of concrete experience. In this sense, they are created by the pressure of circumstances. Thus they are often new; new at least in the sense that the terms are designed to meet the demands of the concrete situation. Probably no one would have thought of this particular settlement except in the setting of the conflict. The American philosopher, Max C. Otto, who was one of the first to analyze and evaluate this process, gave it the apt name of "creative bargaining." The solution is "created" out of all the elements in the conflict situation and in the process of mutual adjustment of the conflicting parties to it. The method of compromise thus works "close to reality." Its attainment is a living process. It is reason at work in the market place, not in the ivory tower. It is men adjusting themselves to one another; not men hugging their pet ideas or fighting about them or sulking in their tents.

A compromise is not a victory for one principle or the other. Principles which are in genuine conflict cannot be reconciled. If either of the principles could have been applied, a settlement would have been easily effected. Principles, unfortunately, are not only abstract but they are usually one-sided. When they are not one-sided, they are likely to be so general as to have no practical utility. Principles usually reflect ideals; and men do not have the same ideals. Insistence upon the application of a categorical principle leaves no alternatives to the partisans of an opposed categorical principle except submission, which is surrender, or resistance by force. In the case of the advocacy of a categorical principle it is "everything or nothing."

Advocacy of the method of compromise is not a doctrine of peace at any price, however. On the contrary, it implies that resistance by force is inevitable when one party insists upon the recognition of the absolute authority of its principle and proposes to enforce this. But this only emphasizes the responsibility of those who propose to take such an uncompromising position. Insistence upon absolute recognition of a principle is clearly an obstacle to the settlement of a human conflict. Yet it is a general human tendency. This is manifested in the habit of announcing principles in preambles, in statements of policy, and in party platforms. Sometimes one or both parties to a compromise insist on the inclusion of a statement of principles, in spite of the fact that the compromise represents a considerable deviation from the principles of all parties concerned.

People who habitually insist on the recognition of absolute principles are often serious obstacles to compromise. Even when they do not finally refuse to compromise, they seriously delay its attainment by obstructionist tactics. The dogmatist is a man who insists on a one hundred per cent recognition of his principle. The insistence by a private citizen on the right to this implies a denial of the same privilege to him who holds an opposite principle. The dogmatist would rather sacrifice a small concrete advance of his cause than "give up his principle." Dogmatists not only delay the solution of human conflicts but also increase the tension which a conflict inevitably generates.

Uncompromising insistence on the recognition of a principle involves the assumption of great moral responsibility. Such responsibility should be based on more solid ground than personal conviction. There must be other authority than that of the conviction of the dogmatist to justify his dogmatism. Yet the individual most dangerous to the peaceful solution of human conflicts is the dogmatist who claims objective authority for his principles and who considers himself to be the personification of such authority. In an emotionally unbalanced personality, such assurance breeds fanaticism. The fanatic entertains no doubts as to the absolute rightness of his convictions, and, if he is in a position of power, brooks no limitation of his authority. A fanatic is the personification of the principle of tyranny.

The acceptance of the necessity of compromise is a recognition of the basic principle of democracy. The purpose of a democratic society is the corporate promotion of all the ends of all the members of that society; not one member's ends only, nor one end completely. Thus in the case of conflict, the purpose of settlement is to attain the greatest possible recognition and furtherance of all the interests of all the individuals involved in the conflict. The interests of the individuals must never be lost sight of. Because compromise implies respect for individual "rights," it works towards a solution by balancing, adjusting, and reconciling conflicting conceptions of these rights.

\* \* \*

It is obvious that compromise as a basic procedural principle of political behavior is unacceptable to the authoritarian, who is the counterpart of the dogmatist in the realm of action. To be sure, he may occasionally "compromise with necessity," but he will refuse to recognize this method of settling conflicts as a necessary rule of procedure. In answer to the objection that social order requires the assertion and application of absolute principles, the proponent of compromise will ask: Yes, but whose principles? And on whose authority? And where are these principles to be found?

A more moderate and practical objection to the method of compromise comes from those who are willing to admit that it is difficult to defend the absolute authority claimed for dogmatic principles but who nevertheless feel that without them no orderly and secure government can be established. The sensible thing to do, according to these critics, is to select the most appropriate and promising principles and use them as permanent controls. Without commitment to some dogmatic principles, a government, as well as any organization or institution, will have no political direction; it will, in fact, have no moral direction. It will be like a ship without a rudder, completely at the mercy of the winds and currents of the moment. To adopt the method of compromise is to surrender to opportunism.

The charge of opportunism is serious and disturbing. The notion of a society in which men habitually conform to the demands of the moment cannot have much appeal for a thoughtful person. But is opportunism the necessary implication of the doctrine of compromise? Opportunism in the sense intended by the critics means complete adaptation to the present opportunity without reference to any except the immediate consequences. It means that action is directed by the thought of immediate profit or advantage. Negatively defined, it is the policy of action without reference to *principles*. An opportunist is commonly taken to be an unprincipled person.

To characterize the doctrine of compromise as opportunistic in this sense is to misrepresent or misunderstand it. In the first place, to compromise is not to ignore principles but to settle a conflict between them. A compromise is a solution in which something has been saved of all the principles in conflict. It is not a denial of one or the other principle but a recognition of the right of all the principles to be heard. The doctrine of compromise insists that the categorical assertion and application of a principle is not an end in itself, to which the furtherance of all other ends must be subordinated, but that principles are intended to be applied in concrete situations; to be used, therefore, as means to an end. When two principles are in conflict, both have a right to be considered because both represent human beings. The purpose of adjustment and conciliation and compromise is to adjust the differences between these human beings and to enable them to continue to live in security and peace and decency with one another. If critics insist that an "absolute" principle must be applied in the settlement of conflicts, let it be the principle that every human being should be given the greatest possible opportunity to realize his own needs, desires, and interests, or the principle that no principle has a right to demand complete and exclusive recognition merely because it is categorical or absolute.

To identify the method of compromise with opportunism is wrong for another reason. To settle a conflict by compromise is not an isolated act, having reference only to the immediate present and divorced from the recorded past and the anticipated future. To conceive of a compromise situation as a moment of self-contained human experience, separated from the antecedent experience of other human beings, from the smaller or larger social settings in which human experience occurs, and from all consideration of the effects of the present action on future experiences, is to entertain a fiction. Neither the individuals nor the issues are disconnected from the past.

The citizens are morally experienced and, to some extent at least, morally mature individuals. In the application of the method of compromise to a conflict, this experience is put to use. Compromises are made by people who know what they want but who also know that it is unlikely that their wants alone will be recognized. If they believe in democracy, they will agree that they are not entitled to this. They will neither, like children, wilfully demand to have their way nor, like savages, resort to brute force.

They will also have learned what the public consequences of private and group selfishness are likely to be. They will have learned this from their own experience as well as from that of their forebears. Both in the matter of methods and principles of settlement, a democratic society possesses an inheritance of human experience. The lessons of the past are recorded in the realm of government as well as in the more general realm of basic and pervasive human relations. These lessons will be in the form of principles of varying degrees of generality and these principles will be in part formally recorded in the law and in part informally embodied in everyday conduct.

The method of compromise is therefore not a surrender to opportunism if by opportunism is meant complete indifference to principles in the settlement of human conflicts. In making this charge, the critic falls into the common polemical error of forcing a choice between two extremes. In this case, the forced alternatives are the acceptance of absolute principles and the denial of all principles. The critic would have us choose between the necessity of applying a principle categorically or applying no principle at all. It is assumed that conflicts must be settled either in bulk by applying a principle whose authority is accepted as absolute or by effecting an isolated adjustment of each particular conflict. In the latter case, the adjustment of the difficulty would have no basis in the past and no authority for the future. Its only justification would be its current acceptability to the parties in conflict.

\* \* \*

The democratic doctrine of compromise implies that both dogmatism and opportunism are wrong. The assumption that in the adjustment of human relations man must choose between the categorical and mechanical application of an absolute principle and the atomism of discrete and disconnected particular solutions is as unreasonable as the assumption that man must choose between tyranny and chaos. The assumption is the result of a misunderstanding of the relation between principle and a particular instance of application. Neither can be considered without reference to the other. The applicability of the principle is not independent of the instances to which it is to be applied; nor are the instances independent of the reference and dominance of the principle. A wholly inapplicable principle is of no use to human beings who have to live concrete lives. Henry van Wesep's "We should not have ethical ends entirely beyond our means" is a wise observation. On the other hand, a world in which there were no principles would be unintelligible. The simplest moral proposition becomes meaningless, however, if divorced from its concrete meaning. "Stealing is wrong" means nothing unless we know what acts constitute stealing. The "wrongness" refers to a particular kind of act and the term "kind of act" has no concrete meaning except with reference to particular acts.

The relationship between principle and particular instance of application is a reflexive one: principle and instance qualify one another. The practical and thus the *real* meaning of a principle is determined by its applications. When the applications of a principle change, the meaning of the principle changes. During periods of unchallenged acceptance, the application to particular instances may be almost automatic. But principles develop out of experience: they are man's ways of ordering human behavior and human relationships. Since experience is never complete, this is a continuous process. Man records and manifests what he has learned in the application of principles.

As has been pointed out above, when principles are recorded they have a tendency to become static. When they are expressed in words, they acquire permanent meanings, permanent in the sense of settled and accepted reference. The meaning of a concept or principle becomes static when its concrete reference becomes finally established. Established reference may fail to include specific cases which seem to be included in the meaning of general idea. Thus we find that people accepted slavery at the same time that they professed belief in the concept of liberty. Sometimes a principle is applied to concrete instances which clearly do not fall within the meaning of the principle. Sometimes principles which in the abstract seem complementary or correlative conflict in the area of concrete application.

The practical problem is therefore the determination of the meaning of a principle by its concrete applications. The abstract concept or principle is like an ideal, the full realization of which can only be approximated, never fully attained. Ideals, though they are in one sense derived from experience, are in another sense products of the human imagination in search of perfection. They represent imaginary not realizable conditions of existence. Men should neither ignore them nor insist that they be completely realized in practice. In its attempts to solve the problem of human life, the intelligence should shuttle to and fro between the ideal world and the real world, forming the real as much after the ideal as possible, evaluating the real in terms of the ideal, and keeping the ideal meaningful and useful by measuring its adaptability to the real. The ideal should neither be despised nor cherished solely as an object of theoretical contemplation or of worship. The real should neither be ignored nor accepted as the ultimate.

It is because men entertain different conceptions of the proper relation of the ideal and the real that social conflicts arise. Men differ in their ideals, or, if they have the same ideals, in their conceptions of how and to what extent they are to be realized. From the standpoint of the democratic state, it is the citizens themselves who must in the last analysis settle their differences on these issues. It is the citizens who must transmute their ideals into workable social and political controls. To do this they must be willing to adjust their differences; they must be willing to apply the method of compromise. If they do so, they will gradually work out practicable applications of principles. Their compromises will be pilot studies in self-government. In the language of the definition of democracy, they will then develop effective corporate means for the realization of their private ends.

\* \* \*

Are there no limits to compromise? It is obvious that whatever may be the demands of the theory, the practice of compromise is limited by the realities of existence. Some men seem congenitally incapable of compromise. They pass from one bitter conflict to another, always seeking to avoid adjustment and conciliation, perpetually frustrated, cut off from cooperation with their fellows, and contributing nothing to the improvement of human relations, though profiting much, in spite of themselves. The professional dogmatist, too, sets at least temporary limits to compromise by insisting on a policy of everything or nothing. The perfectionist, also likely to be a kind of dogmatist, though a worthy and tolerable variety, usually objects to compromising, even with necessity, and consequently seriously limits the practice of compromise. There is also the dogmatist's opposite, the professional anti-authoritarian, who is opposed to all limitation of personal privilege, and thus to all authority, including that which is established by mutual agreement. What he does in fact is to deny all authority except his own, though possibly without realizing it.

The advocate of compromise is likely to be completely helpless if one of the parties in actual or potential conflict has the power to enforce his own will. Not many men or nations are wise and humane enough to compromise with weakness. The temptation to demand submission instead of respecting rights and interests is rarely resisted. The reliance on power and the resort to the authority it gives induce the victims to insure themselves against future domination by acquiring power for themselves. Centralization of power breeds revolt against itself. There is no answer to tyranny but revolution, for compromise is helpless in the presence of arrogant power. It is for this reason that the citizens of a democracy must prevent a potentially dangerous concentration of power in their government. Distribution of power sufficient to serve effectively as a system of checks and balances is a first principle of democratic organization. Where power is equally distributed, compromise is the logical and the "natural" way of solving conflicts.

Assuming the existence of a democratic state, must every conflict be resolved by compromise? It is obvious that there should be no compromise on the issue of the authority of the law. Once a corporate decision has been made, the citizens must submit. If any compromise is to be made in its enforcement, that is the function of the courts, not the right of the individual citizen. To advocate the right of disobedience or private interpretation is to advocate potential political and social chaos. Such advocacy implies that citizens are not bound by public agreements and that commitments of the citizens to corporate ends are not binding on their private ends. To make obedience to law a matter of individual choice is to destroy the state.

The requirement of obedience to the law suggests another requirement which the citizens of a democracy must accept, namely, submission to the accepted compromise. If conflicting parties have agreed on a settlement of their differences, all parties involved in the compromise are committed to observe its terms. If a compromise has been embodied in a law, it must be obeyed because it is the law. If it is a private contract, the laws of contract prescribe the obligation of the contracting parties. A citizen has the privilege of requesting a court to give him relief from what he thinks is an unjust contract. He does not have the right to repudiate a contract unless such a contract was clearly illegal. Likewise, he does not have the right to refuse to abide by a legitimate compromise upon which he or his representatives have agreed. The recognition of the right to compromise implies the prescription of the duty to abide by it.

This interest of the law in compelling men to abide by their private agreements presupposes a prior interest in the kinds of agreements which men make with one another. As has already been suggested, the law forbids men to make compromises or any other kinds of agreements which are not in harmony with specific laws or with accepted general principles of justice. Citizens do not have the right to make compromises which "compromise" the legally defined rights of individuals, including the parties to the compromise. Nor are competing institutions permitted to compromise their differences if thereby the public welfare is endangered. Although compromises frequently point the way to new laws, they must in the first instance be within the law.

To insist that there may be no compromise in the matter of obedience to law is in no sense a denial of the principles of democracy; on the contrary, it is an affirmation of them. Obedience to law is obedience to the will of the people, for they are the political source of the law in a democratic state. To permit disobedience implies either the denial of the authority of all law or the substitution of some other authority for that of the law. It leaves the individual wholly free to substitute his own principles and his own methods for those to which democracy is committed. Each individual then becomes the law. This implies repudiation of the first great principle of democratic government, representativeness.

Insistence on obedience to law is not an autocratic principle, for in a democracy no particular law is held to be absolute. The requirement of submission does not imply that those opposed to the law have no right to attempt to induce their fellow-citizens or their political representatives to change or repeal the law. A democratic state not only formally recognizes this right but provides machinery for effecting whatever changes the citizens may desire to make. The right to make the law implies the right to change it. A vote of the citizens or of their representatives is not the last word on the subject. An election in a democracy is not an enthronement, either of a person or a principle. It is not the voice of infallible authority but the voice of fallible human beings. These fallible beings have the right to change their minds, to correct their mistakes, or even to make new ones. The law must not only *be* representative, it must also *remain* representative. There must therefore be no compromise on the right of the citizen to vote to change the law. To deny this right is to repudiate the second great characteristic of democracy, namely self-correction. Certainly, the processes of democracy are not designed for the purpose of abolishing democracy.

PART II THE MACHINERY OF
DEMOCRATIC GOVERNMENT

SEVEN

# The Role of the Representative

IN THE SENSE THAT DEMOCRATIC GOVERNMENT HAS FOR ITS purpose the greatest possible realization of the ends of the citizens, it is itself a great compromise. How could such a complex purpose be realized except through the medium of adjustment and conciliation? The laws already represent accepted adjustments between conflicting interests of the citizens. Members of the legislative branch of the government are responsible for making new laws or changing old ones, that is to say, for making new adjustments. All public officials are directly or indirectly representatives of the people. They are the agents through whom the transformation of private ends into public ends is accomplished.

The principle of representation, as a matter of fact, is itself a case of compromise, a practical procedural compromise with necessity. In a pure or absolute democracy, that is, in one in which the citizen participated personally in the making of laws and their enforcement, there would be no representatives. There would be no need of them. But pure democracy, if it is possible at all, is not practical when there are a large number of citizens. It would be too cumbersome and slow-moving. If the political group is of any size, not only must the citizens function through representatives but, because of the complexity of problems of government, they must also

## The Role of the Representative

have experts to conduct its business. Democracies differ considerably with respect to degree and character and complexity of representation, as they do with respect to constitutions. But all modern democracies are representative governments.

The idea of representation as such seems simple enough. For many people it means no more than that a candidate for office is elected by the vote of the citizens. Election does indeed determine who is to be the representative; but it does not determine the nature of the relation between the citizens and their public officials. This relationship is conceived in many different ways by people who are otherwise agreed in their support of democratic government. This difference is a matter of great importance, for it involves the question of the rights of the citizens on the one hand and the responsibilities of the public officials on the other.

It has been maintained by some idealistically inclined proponents of democracy that there would be no difference of opinion about the nature of representatives, if all the citizens would only vote in accordance with "the public interest" or "the common good." This point of view is based upon the assumption that there exists an identifiable public interest. Unfortunately, this notion of the public interest is an abstraction, at least in so far as real political conflicts are concerned. In its most ideal manifestation, political conflict is a conflict between competing conceptions of "what is good for the country." Actually, political conflicts represent a complex struggle between a variety of notions held by private individuals and private groups concerning their *private* good. The citizens also hold different notions concerning the ways and means by which their interests are to be furthered. It is these facts which account for the differences of opinion concerning representativeness and the relation between voters and public officials.

A knowledge of these differences of opinion is essential to an understanding of political democracy in action. There are a small minority of citizens who believe that, to be representative, the public official needs only to possess a rare and somewhat mysterious qualification: a high degree of concentration of "the spirit of democracy." He must be a "true democrat," a "real American." It is implied that, given this qualification, he will know what is good for the country and how this good can be accomplished. To use a favorite phrase, the future of the country will be safe in his hands. In his campaign for election, such a candidate needs to do little more to prove his fitness than to pledge himself to uphold the principles and traditions of democracy. The voters are much influenced by the personal appeal of the candidate, and particularly by the emotional quality of his professions. The authority of the representative, like his wisdom, is conceived to be independent of those whom he represents. It is not his duty to further the interests of the voters as they conceive them but as the "spirit of democracy" directs.

In a somewhat less mystical and more tangible variation of this general notion the representative is expected to obtain his political guidance from the Constitution. It is his duty to govern in accordance with its principles and the recorded interpretations of it as represented by "the law." On occasion he has a perfect right to ignore the demands of the voters that he protect and promote their interests. His responsibility is to the Constitution, as he—and not the voters—interprets it. By the act of election, the voters confer this authority on him.

There is another conception which also emphasizes the independence of the elected representative but for a quite different reason. According to this point of view, the legislator does not have authority because he knows best, though this may be the case, but because he has been elected. Power and authority have been *delegated* to him. It is in this sense that his authority is representative. Although the voters will ultimately hold him responsible and pass judgment on his record in a later election, for the period of incumbency he has the right to make his own decisions.

The notion that public officials are not responsible to the citizens but to "something else" is not without danger. It may easily develop into an autocratic conception of government; in fact, it represents a trend in that direction. We have but to recall that the absolute monarch based his royal authority on the fact that he ruled by divine right and was therefore responsible only to God. In the philosophy of National Socialism, Hitler represented the "racial genius" of the German people and allegedly took his instructions from it. In the faith of the traditional Communist, the political policies of the Communist state obey a law of history. In none of these political philosophies is the public official responsible to the citizens in the democratic sense of the term.

The conviction that responsibility to the citizens is, on the contrary, the essence of the democratic principle of representativeness is the general characteristic of another type of opinion. A representative is elected because he stands for the promotion of certain specific ends of the citizens or for certain specific means of realization of these ends. These objectives were announced by the candidate as his policies previous to election and were known to the citizens. The candidate's election is due to the fact that the voters selected his policies rather than those of rival candidates. The candidate is committed to these objectives for the period of his incumbency. He does not merely represent "the people" or "the public interest"; he represents the particular interests and opinions of the voters who elected him.

A first difference among those who accept this general principle has to do with the directness of representation and responsibility. Many proponents of democracy believe that the interposition of a political party between citizens and government is the only practical way of making and keeping elected officials representative of the wishes of the citizens. The virtues of representation through the agency of a political party are these: it is committed and remains committed to a definite set of policies, each of which represents some end or ends of the citizens; it has organization and can therefore act effectively; it has control over candidates; it can direct and, if necessary, discipline them. Political parties represent groups of citizens who have united because they have the same political interests. In short, it brings order out of the variety and confusion of ends entertained by the unorganized mass of the citizens.

Others are of the opinion that party organization is of much more advantage to the politicians than to the citizens. It frequently substitutes interests of the party for those of the citizens. The organization and discipline of the party are obtained at the expense of representation of the differences in interests of the citizens. The unity of the party is a forced and therefore false unity; actually, a party represents almost as great a complex of interests as does the unorganized mass of the voters. The party system is a necessary evil at best; it would be much better if the citizens would not commit themselves to parties, for in doing so they permit too many of their private interests to be ignored or modified.

But who then must a representative represent? And what must he represent? There are those who think that a representative should as far as possible represent all the wishes of all his constituents. It is his duty to see to it that all shall have a hearing in the councils of the government. It is a foregone conclusion that all the ends of all the citizens cannot be realized. He knows that; and, presumably, so do the citizens. It is his business to consult with his colleagues, who have the same assignment as he, and to determine what is the best that can be done under the circumstances. The best is what is fairest for everybody, that is to say, what is the most representative. The representative represents all the people all the time, and not merely his own constituents. The representative from the Sixth District of the State of X is responsible not only for the welfare of the citizens of his district but for the citizens of all other districts. It cannot be otherwise, for he votes on all legislation, not merely on legislation affecting the Sixth District.

According to another point of view the extent and scope of representativeness vary with the nature of the legislation which is under consideration. If the representative's own constituents have a special interest in a legislative proposal, he is in duty bound to promote this, even if he himself does not favor it. To be sure, he is not by law forbidden to vote against the wishes or the interests of his constituents, but if he does so, the constituents have a right to feel that he has violated a political trust. In the case of legislation which does not affect his constituents, he is free to follow his own judgment. Proponents of this view agree, of course, that the scope of representativeness depends upon the office: for example, a

United States Senator represents all the people of his state; a Representative is responsible only to his own district.

According to still another view, the notion that any representative can represent all the voters even of his district, no matter how small the area, is pure fiction. Even if it should miraculously happen that all the voters were agreed on one issue, they would be sure to disagree on another one. A legislator must take sides in every conflict. He must therefore represent the interests of some group. Every representative is on every issue the spokesman of a "special interest." Since many different issues arise, he does not always represent the same group; this depends upon the character of the legislation under consideration. In the case of federal support of education he may represent the religious views of his constituency; in the case of labor legislation, he may represent their labor views. When the alignment between special interests becomes more or less permanent, he may become definitely committed to one interest or another; he may become a "labor senator," for example, or a "big business senator."

Many believers in democracy are opposed to the doctrine that a representative should be committed to special interests. The most significant objection comes from those who insist that this is contrary to the principles of democracy, expressed and implied. Citizens of the United States, for example, point out that the Constitution provides for representation in terms of numbers and geographical areas, and that there is nothing in the Constitution which even indirectly suggests that representation should be based on occupation, profession, economic class, religious affiliation, etc. To advocate this is dangerous, for it will tend to make the political thinking of the citizens narrowly partisan: every citizen will judge every legislative issue in terms of the special interests of the group or groups to which he belongs. The unity of the nation will be seriously endangered by this kind of political thinking. The citizens should be taught and encouraged to think in terms of the good of the whole, that is, in terms of broad, national policies.

There is another objection which deserves consideration. It is argued that if the elected representatives of the citizens are to be nothing more than the mouthpieces of special interests, their election is a waste of time. It would have saved time if the citizens had voted directly on the issues instead of on representatives. This objection does not have much to commend it, though its consideration will serve to bring out some significant implications of the democratic doctrine of representation. The proponents of the objection forget several important facts. First there is the important fact that a legislative body is a deliberative body and is the forum in which current political issues are publicly discussed, to the enlightenment not only of the representatives but also of their constituents. The deliberations of such a body and the consequent public report and evaluation of them constitute a most important source of information, both for the nation and for other countries.

In the second place, there is the fact that at best only a very limited number of issues are involved in any particular election. Many more issues develop in the Congress of the United States, for example, than are discussed in an election. Moreover, new issues arise between elections and on these the representative will not have been instructed. Even on those which have been campaign issues the commitments of candidates are in some cases certain to have been general or vague. The citizens, on their part, are prone to vote on the general political attitude of the candidate or that of his party, or on the personality of the candidate, or on a dozen and one factors which have no connection with the issues. This confusion is worse confounded by politicians who often purposely conceal their position on crucial issues or raise irrelevant but politically effective pseudo-issues.

It is for these reasons that some proponents of democracy insist that to make government representative it is essential to assure continued sensitivity of public officials to the wishes of the citizens. The government must be kept representative between elections. The relation of representation between citizen and the successful candidate is not terminated by the fact of election. It is therefore necessary for the citizens, individually or in groups, to keep informing their representatives of their wishes. The formation of pressure groups and lobbying are the best means of doing this.

Defense of lobbying and pressure groups does not imply that the citizens are not limited with respect to the means to be employed in exerting influence on the legislators. They are restricted in a legal sense by laws which they themselves have passed for this purpose. Citizens are forbidden to buy votes and to bribe legislators, for these practices make a commodity of the vote and a hireling of the legislator. This practice destroys the proper democratic relationship of representation between the citizen and the legislator. By implication, the buyer owes the seller nothing more, until there is a further purchase. The buyer has resigned the right to have his interest considered free of charge. The economic relation of buyer and seller is a monetary relationship, determined by the accident of possession. It is terminated by the passing of cash. The relation of representation, on the contrary, is established by conscious selection. It is a stable one and can be terminated only by an election.

The practice of buying votes is also corrupting and therefore wrong in a general moral sense. Both seller and buyer fail to act as morally responsible persons. The criterion of moral responsibility is free choice. No lower estimate can be placed on a moral decision than a cash value. (Of course, in bribery cash is not the only medium of exchange). Finally, the practice is wrong because both the purchase of a vote and the bribery of a legislator destroy political equality. The citizen who has the most money will have the greatest purchasing power and thus the greatest political power. Money must not be accepted as the measure of political power. The right to a vote is the right of a person. The citizen, not his wealth, is the political entity.

There is one other conception of the function of the elected representative which must be considered. Its central idea is that it is not the primary function of the representative to make conflicts but to solve them. He can do this best by functioning as a conciliator. To be sure, ultimately he will have to act also as umpire, since he will have to vote on whatever legislation may be proposed. His first duty, however, is to serve as a mediator between the special interests in conflict and try to induce them to accept a compromise. The exact character of this function has been effectively described by one of its leading exponents, T. V. Smith. When leaders of pressure groups approach their representatives, says Professor Smith, each is determined to fight to the bitter end for the interest he represents. He is determined not to give an inch in the struggle. Usually, he is convinced that the issue is a matter of principle and that, since he is a man of principle, he is morally bound to stand by his principles. He is sorry, but he simply cannot compromise on matters of principle. What determines the task of the representative—and what makes it so difficult—is the fact that other parties to the conflict are also men (or women) of principle. Now it is obvious that no law can be devised which will embody all the conflicting principles or grant all the rights which are allegedly claimed on their authority. It may be unfortunate, but it is a fact that the complete recognition of the rights of one party means a complete denial of the opposite party.

Since the legislator is the representative of all his constituents, and in a sense of all the constituents of all his colleagues, he is not justified in being partisan. He represents people, not principles. He must therefore try to reconcile these claims. There is only one way of doing this: to induce the parties in conflict to accept something less than they claim. When this is accomplished, by "creative bargaining" on the part of the representatives of the special interests, wisely and skillfully directed by the legislator, the conflict will have been solved in true democratic fashion. It is true that the politician will be the scapegoat, for he will be blamed by all parties as responsible for the failure of the "government" to recognize rights and to support principles. However, citizens will have been induced to recognize one another's rights. Human beings will have been influenced to settle their differences peacefully. Thus the fundamental purpose of democracy will have been realized, namely, the satisfaction of as many ends of as many citizens as possible.

Critics of this conception have raised the point that the private interests in conflict ought to settle their differences privately and effect private compromises. If they did this, there would be no need of the services of representatives; there would not even be need of legislation. There are several reasons why citizens so often fail to try to settle conflicts privately and why, when they do try, they are so often unsuccessful. In the first place, human beings rarely seem able to be sufficiently objective to appreciate the necessity and the practical advantages of compromise. They are carried away by selfishness and misled by the hope, not always wholly vain, of attaining their ends in full. In this selfishness they are encouraged by an equal selfishness in their fellows; in fact, they deliberately organize in order to promote their selfishness systematically. Individual selfishness is nourished by group selfishness and the hope of success is strengthened.

In the second place, they often do not know how to reach a compromise, because they have not enough knowledge with respect to the issues and potential consequences of alternative solutions. It cannot be expected, for example, that in a capital-labor dispute the representative of either party will have sufficient knowledge of economics, pure or applied, to determine the consequences of the solutions which they demand. This does not imply that we should expect every conflict to be settled in accordance with the judgment of experts. Even experts do not always have sufficient information to give wise counsel to the parties in conflict, and, even if they did, such wisdom may be powerless against selfishness and against the contentiousness and bitterness which are generated by a conflict. This suggests a third obstacle to the attainment of a compromise by the contesting parties, namely, the lack of psychological skill of the average citizen in the conduct of human relationships which will be productive of compromise, their lack of skill, specifically, in the social techniques of conciliation and negotiation. Most people are not compromise minded; they have had insufficient training in the technique of adjustment and conciliation to have developed within themselves an attitude of mind which is compounded of a confirmed conviction of the need of compromises and of the will to promote and accept them.

For these reasons, and because the parties in a conflict always expect action in favor of their interests, legislators and legislative bodies become involved in conflicts of interests.

The public assumes that these conflicts can be much more easily solved by the representatives of the people than by the people themselves. Are representatives not chosen because they know how to govern? Are members of legislative bodies not elected because they know what laws should be passed? If the people are split into conflicting groups, each with its own special interest, the legislator should certainly be able to find a compromise which would represent the most effective realization of the ends of all the rival parties. If he believes in democracy—and this may certainly be assumed—he should be willing to do this. If he has offered himself for election, he should be able to do so.

\* \* \*

When we examine political life as it is lived in a real democracy, it is evident that concrete political practice does not represent any one of these conceptions of representativeness exclusively but is a mixture of all of them. Not only do the citizens and their representatives have different views but they change their views with the issues. A citizen will, quite innocently, condemn a legislator for refusing to compromise in one case and for agreeing to do so in another. He will commend his own representative for diligent promotion of the interests of his own group but condemn the representative of the opposition for doing the same for his neighbor's organization. But it is, after all, these human tendencies for which democracy makes provision in theory and practice. It is the variety and complexity and rivalry and competition of human interests that helps to keep democratic society in equilibrium. There is, therefore, no reason why the believer in democracy should be forced to choose between the conception of the representative as an independent leader or as a slavish follower. In actual practice, the public official is a mixture of leader and follower. He is an element in the complex of democratic political society. His responsibility may differ from that of the ordinary citizen in character and degree but in the last analysis it is the same in essence: to help effect the greatest possible realization of the ends of the citizens.

Too much stress therefore cannot be laid on the responsibility of the political representative in a democracy. The fact of election has concentrated in him the responsibility of all those whom he represents. The number of citizens whose responsibility he directly bears depends upon the size of his constituency. This varies from that of the representative of a relatively small group of citizens in a sparsely populated district to that of the President of the United States, who represents all the citizens of the country. The vote of a representative in the legislative body of a small municipality may represent only a handful of voters. The decision of the President of the United States currently represents that of about sixty million.

The vote of a representative in a democracy usually involves the welfare of many more people than he technically represents. When a legislator casts a vote in settlement of a conflict between special interests, his vote affects many people who are not active participants in the dispute. When conflicts develop between special interests, there are always "innocent bystanders." In industrial conflicts, the welfare of some proportion of the general public is always involved. Even if the legislators have been elected by labor or capital or on a labor or capital platform, they are not justified in ignoring the interests of the general public.

It might be affirmed that if a representative is elected by a special interest, he is politically committed to vote for that interest and that the consequences are the responsibility of those who elected him. It may possibly be granted that this is a defensible position in a narrow and strictly formalistic political sense. It must be insisted, however, that his position is, in the first place, not morally defensible. No citizen, whether he holds political office or not, can justify indifference to the welfare of his fellow citizens, be they few or many. In the second place, it reflects an immature social philosophy and a failure to understand the nature of social conflicts and their solution. A partisan vote for a special interest is a categorical decision in favor of one interest and against another. It is a vote in favor of dominance of one right, not of the recognition of mutual rights. Such a vote is not in harmony with the basic democratic doctrine of compromise. It conceives of the representative as a mere perpetuator of private conflict with no responsibility except to promote the private interests which he represents. Such a conception of political responsibility obviously ignores the function of public officials in a democratic government, namely, the greatest possible promotion of the interests of all the citizens.

Because of the nature of democratic government, there is no single answer to the question of responsibility in a representative government. The king's commissioner has only to execute the royal will. The commissar is the all-powerful representative of an autocratic authority outside of and above the people and is provided with many of his decisions ready-made. In a democracy, the representative is under several compulsions, a compound of the will of his constituents (which is often several wills), the public welfare, and his own conscience. He is under one other compulsion which, fortunately, is a unifying influence, namely, *to govern in accordance with the principles and procedures of democratic government.* The representative is more than a private citizen; more than a representative of some or all of his constituents; more than a member of a political party; more than a guardian of the public welfare; he is an agent of democratic government. As such he is committed to promote the solution of conflicts in the democratic way.

*EIGHT*

## Government by Majority

THE ELECTION OF REPRESENTATIVES AND OTHER OFFICIALS OF the government represents the first stage in the solution of conflicts in a democracy. The decisions of these officials and their appointees represent the second, and, in a relative sense, final stage. Continuity in varying degrees between the will of the people and the decisions of the government is formally established and maintained by means of popular elections. Because of the complexity and variety of the demands of the citizens, the policies of a democratic government at any time are only an approximation of the will of the people. General suffrage and frequent elections are the means devised to assure the best approximation. General suffrage assures the expression of the greatest possible variety of opinion, whether it be the expression of wisdom or folly, of knowledge or ignorance, of fair judgment or bias.

If an election is to settle anything, however, there must be some rule of procedure, previously agreed upon, for determining whose opinion is to prevail. The rule of the majority is the universal by-law of all democratic institutions, political and non-political. In a democratic state, representatives are elected and laws are passed by majority vote. In the courts, guilt or innocence is determined by a majority vote of the judges or jury, unless the law provides otherwise. In the case of compromises, though they represent the maximum in agreement, the final decision is usually that of the majority. In the Supreme Court of the United States, even the meaning of the Federal Constitution is determined by majority vote.

Citizens of a democracy take this majority principle for granted and think little about its origin or justification; yet it must at one time have been a subject of much discussion. After having decided that the governed should determine how they were to be governed, it must have been disturbing and embarrassing to find so many different notions among the governed as to how this was to be done. Some rule of procedure had to be adopted which could be consistently applied, first, in the business of founding the government and, secondly, in the more difficult task of perpetuating it. Since unanimity was seen to be a false hope and minority rule seemed unreasonable, rule by the majority was the only sensible solution.

Before inquiring into the implications and assumptions of the rule by the majority principle, it should be noted, in the first place, that the term does not have a single constant quantitative meaning. The size of the majority prescribed ranges from a bare majority of one to as high a fraction as four-fifths. This is a subject of perennial dispute: the problem is to maintain the majority principle and at the same time to assure a "representative" majority and thus to guard against government by too small a percentage of the voters. In the second place, in a democratic state there are practices which are deviations from this rule. Some of these do not seem to violate the principle of quantitative representativeness; others clearly do. Although the members of the United States Senate are elected by majority vote, a vote of the entire membership of this body may not, in fact, represent the will of the majority of the citizens of the country, even if each senator expresses the will of the majority of his constituents. The explanation lies in the fact that each state in the Union is assigned two seats in the Senate, no matter how large or how small the population of that state. In consequence, a majority of the senators may actually represent a minority of the voting population at large. This majority will, however, represent a majority of the states as political units, and that is, of course, exactly what the founding fathers intended. Since the United States is a republic, it was felt that the units of this republic should be represented as such. The underlying purpose of checks and balances which this serves is too well known to require discussion here. There is little if any objection to this policy, particularly because it is balanced by representation by majority in the other legislative body, the House of Representatives.

There is, on the contrary, persistent objection, now taking the form of a proposal to amend the Constitution, to the fact that the Electoral College system of choosing a President actually makes it possible for a minority of the citizens to elect the President of the United States. An analogous situation obtains in other political units: in the state of Georgia, for example, a minority can elect the Governor of the state. In view of the doubts of proponents of democracy about the propriety of this comparatively minor deviation from the principle of representativeness, it is not surprising that they consider a travesty on democracy the current situation in Russia, where the members of the one controlling Communist party constitute less than four per cent of the total population of the United Soviet Republics.

\* \* \*

An examination of the majority rule principle reveals certain basic assumptions which are characteristically democratic. The counting of votes by which both majority and minority opinion is determined implies that the casting of a vote is a personal matter. Every vote represents the decision of an individual. The final result is determined by a "counting of noses." It implies, too, that the result could not have been determined in advance, unless the election was not a genuinely democratic one. If there is some form of coercion, there is a denial of the majority rule principle. If, for example, the citizens are not given the opportunity of a free choice between candidates or between alternative policies, the result of the vote will not have the maximum democratic significance. Recent history contains examples of allegedly democratic elections in which the result was predetermined by open or concealed control by the government in power, either by means of manipulation of the election machinery or by intimidation of the voters. When this happens an election is a farce and the government's claim of majority support may be a pretense.

Interference with free elections occurs both in countries which are not genuine democracies, but which for some reason or another wish to pretend to be so, and in those which are genuinely democratic in theory and practice. In the former, there is no escape from autocratic control of elections, except by revolution. In the latter, interference with free suffrage is legally forbidden and is considered a serious crime. A majority is obviously not a majority if it represents minority opinion. In the case of the United States of America, it is true that, as a result of abstention from voting, the majority vote may actually represent only a minority of the citizens. This is possible because abstention from voting in this country is a matter of choice. Such is not the case in all democracies. In some, voting is compulsory and the voter has a choice between voting or paying a fine. The difference in practice represents a difference in point of view with respect to the issues involved, namely, the propriety, from a democratic standpoint, of forcing a citizen to vote, the practicability of general enforcement, the value of a forced vote, and the cumulative effect of compulsion on the attitude of the citizens towards democratic government.

Assuming that a decision is that of a true majority honestly determined, what exactly has been established? Not truth, certainly. Truth cannot be determined by voting. We are reminded here of two state legislatures which reportedly undertook to settle rival claims as to the location of an important historical event by legislative acts, each naturally decreeing that the event took place within its own borders. No less ridiculous was the alleged proposal of a law-maker to have the legislative body of which he was a member pass a bill legally changing the value of the geometrical ratio $pi$ from 3.14159 to 3, the motive being to make the study of geometry easier for school children. Objective truth, that is to say, truth which is independent of the opinion or will of the voters, cannot be established by voting. A historical fact occurred even if the citizens of a country unanimously vote that it did not occur. The laws of nature cannot be determined by the vote of the people any more than they can be determined by the decision of the Politburo.

It is clearly not truth that is established by the rule of the majority. On the contrary, if truth is an issue, a solitary individual may be right and all the rest of his fellowmen wrong. Truth is not established by voting but by demonstration and proof, and these processes are entirely independent of the vote. The "truth" of a vote can be proved only in the sense that it occurred as a fact or in the sense that it was a vote for candidate X. To be sure, the decision represented by a vote may be based on truth in the sense that the individual believes this truth to have been satisfactorily demonstrated. Thus a citizen may vote for a high tariff on the basis of what is to him acceptable economic proof that high tariffs will support high prices for the articles which he is manufacturing, or that they will assure general prosperity to the nation. The vote of the believing citizen, however, does not establish the truth of these propositions: it only records his belief in them.

Most believers in democracy would also deny that moral right and wrong in an ultimate or objective sense can be determined by voting. Yet it cannot be properly denied that voting is, in a very real sense of the term, a moral act. When a citizen casts a vote, he helps to decide a course of action, not only for himself, but for his neighbor. He decides something with respect to the realization of the ends of his fellowcitizens. He votes to extend or to limit their freedom. His vote may be a vote for peace or war. It may help to provide economic security for the underprivileged or it may help to deny them this. It may contribute to the growth of the sense of individual responsibility or to its decline. Since a vote has moral consequences, it represents a moral decision, even if the voter does not realize this.

The same is true for the vote of a majority. It is a moral act because it establishes controls over individuals. The mode of life of some or all of the people is affected. Economic opportunities are expanded or limited. Standards and customs and habits of living are determined. Even habits of thinking are affected. The whole environment in which children are educated and trained may be gradually altered as a result of a trend in public policies. The physical welfare of the people, their attitude toward work, their sense of private and public responsibility, their growth and development, their opportunities for the development of their capacities and for the satisfaction of needs, desires, and interests—for "realization of ends" —are directly affected by the behavior of the public officials who have been elected and by the social and economic policies to which they are committed.

Those who participate in a majority decision certainly bear moral responsibility for it. To deny this would be to absolve men of moral responsibility for the effect of their actions on their fellowmen. It would remove political action from the realm of morality. It would make political life morally irresponsible. It would deprive democracy of its moral character and reduce government to an amoral kind of social mechanics. It would, as a matter of fact, take the moral sense out of political life.

But, if voting is a moral act, does not a majority vote establish a moral principle? Certainly, if the majority of the citizens of a country vote for prohibition, this represents a moral judgment on the liquor traffic. In a democracy, does not such a decision have objective moral authority? Must not all citizens bow to this authority? These questions again assume that moral authority is determined by quantitative superiority. If this were the case, the minority would always be morally wrong. This assumption makes moral right and wrong independent of the moral grounds on which the individual citizens based their decisions. It implies that if it turns out that a citizen voted with the minority, either his moral principles were unsound or his moral reasoning was wrong.

The fundamental error in this reasoning is the identification of moral authority with political and legal authority. In the theory and practice of democracy, an election is not a means of determining what is morally right but how the citizens wish to be governed. It is not a procedure for establishing moral laws but the laws of the state. When a basic democratic document such as the Constitution of the United States is adopted by vote, whether it be unanimously or merely by a majority, the voters determine how and by whom they wish to be governed. They select both political ends and political means. Subsequently, the elections proceed within the framework of the democratic state, as prescribed in the basic law, e.g., the Constitution. They record the consensus of opinion for the purpose of directing the government; they express the continued "consent of the governed." The vote of the majority is merely the prescribed way of deciding who shall be elected to office and what the policies of the elected officials are to be. Defeated candidates and policies are not by virtue of defeat morally wrong; they are simply at the time politically unacceptable to the voters.

The distinction between moral law and law in the legal sense becomes clear if we consider what happens in the trial of a citizen accused of a crime. The decision of the jury is not an ultimate universal moral judgment. If the members of the jury do what the legal system expects them to do, the vote of each member will indicate whether or not he considers the defendant guilty *under the law* of the crime of which he has been accused. The juryman is not expected and, strictly speaking, is not permitted to pass judgment on the goodness or badness of the law. He may, however, do exactly that. Or he may feel that the accused, though guilty, should not suffer the punishment provided for the crime. His vote may indicate that he considers society and not the criminal ultimately responsible for the crime. But if he does this he is setting himself above the law and passing moral judgment upon it.

In political life, likewise, an individual may hold the majority decision to be morally wrong and may, at his risk, refuse to recognize its authority. He may refuse to abide by the Constitution, a law, the verdict of a jury, or the result of an election. In this case, his conviction rests on some principle "outside of" the law of the state, which he considers to be more fundamental and thus to have superior authority. Disobedience of a law may be a moral judgment passed upon a law in terms of some ethical or religious system or conviction to which an individual or institution is committed. This does not deprive the law of its legal and political authority. Mass disobedience of a law is likewise not proof of the fact that the law is morally bad, though it does in fact destroy its authority. Whatever other commitments he may have made, the individual is responsible to the law and thus to the state, and one of the functions of the state is to see that he lives up to this responsibility.

The relation between the vote of the individual citizen and the majority decision is now clear: the opinion or conviction of the individual is not mysteriously transformed by the act of voting into an objective moral pronouncement. It is merely his individual decision which will be counted with the decisions of his fellow citizens in order to determine the distribution of opinion and the nature of the will of the majority. The individual votes of the majority have collectively attained political authority by virtue of the fact that they constituted a majority. In this sense, the decisions of the individual voters have become objectified. Although the authority of this particular decision is not absolute and unchangeable, it is established for the time being and officially prevails until it is withdrawn or changed by the same procedure. If the individual is on the side of the majority he will feel that his will has counted for something; if he is with the minority, he may feel that his will has been disregarded. In either case, he will have to submit to the will of the majority. This is a "law of the game"; it represents a rule of procedure previously agreed upon. It is a basic rule of democracy, and belief in democracy implies a willingness to abide by it. It is one way in which democracy seeks to attain the greatest possible realization of the greatest number of ends of the greatest number of citizens.

\* \* \*

The correctness of the above interpretation of the majority rule principle is borne out by some "brute facts" about majorities. First of all, the fact that the members of the majority voted alike is no certain indication that they did so for the same reason. Voters cast their ballots for the same candidate because they like him personally or because he apparently dislikes the same people they dislike or because he comes from the right family or the right section of the country; because he belongs to the right religion or because his opponent belongs to the wrong one; because he promises to lift the tax on oleomargarine or because he promises to increase the tax on cigarettes; because he is for prohibition; because he is for federal aid to education; or because he is against socialized medicine; and so forth. Agreement thus does not necessarily imply unanimity.

The votes of the majority may be consistent in the sense that they are all the expression of the same political point of view. Even in the case of voters whose decision represents a commitment to a political principle or ideology, to a system of morals, or to a religion, the majority vote may not only represent many different kinds of basic principles and even principles which are themselves hardly compatible, but may even represent incompatible inferences from the same principles. Both voters for and against prohibition believe their votes to be based on Scriptural injunctions. A basic principle may be applied in one case and ignored in another. A citizen may vote for a high tariff because he thinks it to be economically sound and for old age pensions because his religion seems to require this, in spite of the fact that he considers it economically unsound. The height of disharmony and confusion seems attained when a majority favoring stricter labor legislation includes both voters who support it because they think it will bring order into economic life and those who believe it will create economic confusion and thus undermine the stability of the democratic form of government.

There is finally the fact that, although this heterogeneity of opinions is usually unintentional and not even realized by the citizens who constitute the majority, it is not infrequently the result of expert political maneuvering. In the practice known in familiar speech as "horse-trading," the majority is an artificial one and is the result of agreements to exchange votes for the purpose of assuring majorities for bills in which the "traders" have special interests. A and B, neither of whom has any particular interest in the other's pet political project, agree to "trade" support for mutual benefit.

Considerable consistency in the majority is, of course, assured by the party system. It is probably safe to say that most citizens have strong party loyalties and consistently vote for candidates and policies selected or recommended by the party. Since a political party has a platform which usually represents a general political point of view, in accordance with which party leaders choose candidates and take sides on public issues with a considerable degree of consistency, a party majority is to this extent the expression of a high degree of agreement. Unless the members of the party vote merely as and because the party instructs them to do so—a practice which has serious dangers in a democracy—even a party majority, however, is certain to represent many different opinions and convictions, for citizens do not by any means initially choose parties for the same reason.

* * *

The fact that a majority may be itself a combination of minorities or even a complex of incompatible points of view does not represent a nullification of the majority principle, as is sometimes claimed. In a democratic form of government, *some* decision must be reached. An examination of the alternatives to government by majority rule emphasizes its advantages and strengthens our faith in it. Since chaos and dictatorship are not forms of democracy, they are not acceptable alternatives and need not be considered here. One alternative to government by the majority, at least theoretically possible, would be government "by the book"; that is to say, direction and control of public officials by a detailed body of laws comprising instructions and regulations not only for the routine conduct of the government but also for variation of this conduct in response to changing conditions. The notion envisages the existence of an encyclopedic guide for government officials, something analagous to a rule book for a particular sport or a complete handbook for gardeners. It is obvious that this is a romantic and wholly impractical notion, which ignores the facts of social life and fails to understand the sense in which democracy is a continuing process of direction and control of human relations which must be adapted to changing conditions. It assumes that the principles and laws of government can be discovered once and for all. Even if the citizens would continue periodically to change public officials, they would obviously have no part in the determination of policies. Such a form of government, if not in the first instance a modified form of autocracy, would certainly have an inherent affinity for it.

Assuming commitment to a genuine form of democracy, government by the minority would not be an acceptable alternative. Even if it be granted that there is no good reason why the minority should be assumed to be less intelligent, less good, less right, or less wise than the majority, what reason can there be for favoring its judgment over that of the majority? Certainly, there is also no reason for assuming its superiority over the majority in respect to these characteristics. Although it might be difficult to prove this to be a fact, it is generally assumed that there is a probability in favor of the assumption that good sense, or at least the better sense, abides with the majority. Wherever the greater wisdom may dwell, there remains the inescapable and undeniable fact that the wish of the majority is the wish of the greater number of citizens and that government by the majority is therefore more likely to represent the interests of the greatest number of citizens.

An even more practical consideration is the fact that it would be difficult if not impossible to enforce the will of the minority on the majority. It is true that few if any laws are completely enforced. A law passed by the majority will certainly have a better chance of a greater degree of enforcement than a law passed by a minority. It is difficult to enforce a law, even if passed by the majority, when that law does not genuinely express the will of the majority; witness the case of the prohibition law. (When too many of the majority pass a law for the real or supposed good of their neighbors rather than for themselves, the enforcement of that law is not likely to have the complete support of the majority.) There is, finally, the very practical fact that the vote of the majority represents the *will* of the greatest number and thus represents the dominant authority. The minority consequently realizes that the majority has a greater power to enforce than the minority has to resist. From the standpoint of the maintenance of internal order and stability, and domestic peace, more is therefore to be expected of majority rule than of minority rule.

A consideration of the implications of the majority rule principle and alternatives to it and of the constitution of political majorities makes it clear that government by the majority is in itself a compromise. Taking the term democracy in its widest sense, government by the majority lies somewhere between the extremes of government of each individual by himself and government of each individual by all other individuals including himself. The former is not government at all. If the need of government is granted, it is an unacceptable alternative. The latter, if not an impossible alternative, is certainly an impractical one. If unanimity is too idealistic, let us be satisfied with the nearest approach to it. This is what a majority represents.

*NINE*

# The Role of the Minority

IT IS TEMPTING TO ACCEPT THE MAJORITY RULE PRINCIPLE AS A complete answer to the problem of representation and conclude that it is the function of the elected official simply to represent the majority which elected him. To do so would be to ignore some conclusions concerning the nature of political representation and the composition of majorities previously considered. Victory in an election does not confer autocratic authority on the majority. Minorities do not become politically non-existent in consequence of their defeat. An elected public official is not merely the representative of the citizens who elected him; he is also an agent of the government. Since he is a representative of democracy, he is also in some sense or other the representative of the minority. Nothing could be more fundamentally undemocratic than for the majority to demand that its representatives ignore the political existence and political rights of minorities.

In view of the tragic predicament of minorities in contemporary non-democratic political societies, it is particularly relevant to examine the fortunate position of a minority in a true democracy. In an absolute monarchy, where the will of the monarch is the law of the state, disagreement with the will of the monarch in thought or in act is disloyalty. The existence of a minority is not even permitted. Its existence is anticipated, to be sure, as the existence of crime is anticipated; but this implies that the minority lies outside of the law. In an autocracy it is illegal to be a member of a minority whose purpose it is to change the law. To plot against the law in a monarchy is to plot against the king. To organize to change the law—or the ruler—is treason. In the doctrine of rule by divine right, the dissenter by implication dissents from the will of God. In a form of autocratic government in which the policies of government are allegedly predetermined by some force or power or will outside of the state, and thus independent of the citizens, the citizen does not have the right of independent judgment. Opposition not only to the form of government but even to the policies of those who happen to be in power is considered disloyal. To dissent is to revolt against the cosmic purpose or historical destiny of which the autocratic government is the only authorized representative.

It follows that the minority which dissents has not even the right to live. The government not only has the legal right but the moral duty to remove them from the scene. Since a live dissenter is always a potential traitor, it is best to "liquidate" him. Dissenters are obstacles to the realization of the good of mankind—as this is understood by the "liquidators"—and their removal is therefore also morally right. If only those in power *can* be right, all dissenters *must* be wrong. To promote and assist in the removal of those who are wrong is therefore a manifestation of proper moral as well as political responsibility.

In a democracy, it is not disloyal to disagree with the policies of the government. Loyalty and disloyalty are not determined by an election. A citizen is not an enemy of the government by virtue of the fact that he belongs to the minority. In a democracy, on the contrary, minorities are considered an essential part of the "body politic." Not only are they not liquidated, but they are actually protected and encouraged. Provision is often made for them to participate in the government. The minority may be made temporarily powerless by an election, but this does not deprive it of the opportunity of later succeeding to power. It is true that in a democracy political efforts are sometimes made to make a minority permanently powerless; but invariably protectors and defenders arise to defeat this purpose, for those who really understand democracy realize that the existence of minorities is essential to the existence of democracy. In the British democracy, the minority is actually referred to as "His Majesty's Loyal Opposition"! The name implies that dissent with the current policies of the government is perfectly compatible with loyalty.

In some democracies the basic law provides for proportional representation and thus for representation in the government of any minority which makes a respectable numerical showing in the elections. Sometimes there is provision for the government to appoint a representative when a minority fails to muster enough votes to be entitled numerically to such a representative. The actual governing power in such countries is frequently a coalition of minorities. Only in a two-party system of government is the emergence of a majority and the temporary control, or attempted control, of the government by this majority a practical certainty. Even in the two party type of democracy, the minority, though it may not be adequately represented in the government, is a recognized political power. If it is numerically very weak, the party may be politically dormant and its power only potential; but its right to become strong and its opportunity to become dominant are as real as ever, for this right and this opportunity are assured by the basic law.

\* \* \*

What is the reason for this great concern in democracy for minorities? The reason is that minorities play an essential role in the democratic form of government and are therefore an indispensable part of the democratic state. As has already been pointed out, a minority is a minority merely because of its numerical inferiority. It is obvious, therefore, that it may become the majority. If enough members of the majority or of other minorities change their minds in favor of the principles of a minority, that minority becomes the majority. In a democracy, the minority is not necessarily wrong because too few people accept its point of view.

This would not even be the reason for the wrongness of a minority in an autocratic form of government. The reason that there is no place for minorities in an autocratic form of government is the fact that in an autocracy it is assumed that those who are in power are categorically right. They are right because they represent and rule in accordance with political principles which are absolutely right, because that form of government is absolutely right, and because the authority of those who govern in accordance with those principles must necessarily be absolute. When, in addition, the authority to govern has been vested once and for all in some group or succession of persons, the right and duty of that group or succession to provide for the conduct of the government for the future as well as present are also assumed to be absolute. Since in such a form of government a minority must necessarily be in opposition either to the principles of the government or to those who rule in accordance with them, the minority must, by definition, be absolutely wrong. Or, if it is desired to make a distinction between being morally and politically wrong, they are at any rate politically wrong. They are outside of the law and are not entitled to any political rights. This would be true even if the supporters of the minority point of view were numerically in the majority.

The explanation of the great concern about minorities in a democracy is in the last analysis to be found in the basic democratic principle of self-correction. Democracy conceives of government as a continuing experimental social process. It is committed to the indispensability of this process, because it is this process which makes improvement and correction of the actual business of government possible. It is assumed that people as well as conditions change and that there must be corresponding changes in the policies and processes of government. Even if the occurrence of change were not assumed, the need of correction and improvement would still be there, for it is also an implication of political democracy that there are no available or discoverable absolute principles which can be adopted once and for all and forever applied in the business of governing. It follows that there are no absolutely good or expert or reliable political leaders who can be placed permanently in charge of the government. Democracy does not worship change; it is not committed to change for its own sake. Change is accepted as a necessary consequence of the fact that a democratic form of government is government by *human beings*. Since human beings are neither infallible nor unchanging, a government conducted by them or their representatives must provide for change. In view of the fact that a change initiated by the voters is in their opinion always considered to be an improvement or a necessary expedient, we are justified in designating this basic characteristic of democracy as the principle of self-correction.

It is a foregone conclusion that there will be differences of opinion among the citizens as to how this correction is to be effected. They will differ both with respect to policies and officials. Since the citizens select policies and officials by means of elections, it is practically certain that there will always be minorities. Minorities are a natural and necessary part of a democratic society and this is why their existence and protection are provided for in the basic law. Their existence is the principal guarantee of the maintenance of the principle of self-correction. To abolish or suppress minorities is to terminate the democratic process.

This becomes clear if we consider what part minorities play in the political life of a democracy. To begin with, a minority always represents an alternative to the majority party. It stands for a point of view which at the time of election was not accepted by the majority of the voters. This does not mean, necessarily, that the policies of the minority were wrong or undemocratic. As a matter of fact, the minority may ultimately turn out to have been "right," or at any rate more nearly "right" than the majority. The minority point of view may become the point of view of the majority of the voters at the next election. To govern in accordance with its policies is thus always potentially a function of the minority.

It also has some actual and immediate functions to perform in the democratic state. One of these functions is to serve as a critic of the party in power and of its policies and personnel. The minority will keep a sharp eye on the administration of the government by the majority: it will evaluate its policies, measure their success or failure, keep the majority alive to its responsibilities, and generally acquaint the public with what the majority is doing. Minorities are not only by nature critical of the policies of the ruling majority but also of its office holders. For defeated minority candidates to view the public activities of successful candidates with jaundiced eye may serve some useful purpose. Minority candidates will miss no opportunity to remind successful candidates—and the voters—of campaign promises and prophecies. To work under the critical eye of a minority, which is ever ready to say "I told you so," is a salutary situation for the majority.

Minorities are also useful for the purpose of keeping issues alive. They keep the citizens thinking about problems and their solutions. They remind citizens of the fact that there may be other and better ways of solving the country's economic and social problems than those to which they are at the moment committed. They keep the citizens from falling into the "deep slumber of a decided opinion." Active minority leaders will prevent the public from succumbing to the temptation, so dangerous in a democracy, of taking their government for granted. It will be very difficult for "vested interests" to gain control of the government if there are watchful minorities about. Tendencies of policies and officials to become entrenched and in consequence to develop autocratic characteristics will be exposed by jealous minorities, for entrenchment of power is a threat to the existence of minorities.

Minorities are also useful because they frequently "force the issue." They compel the majority to come out into the open with unpopular policies or to explain the meaning and implications of broad platform declarations or to take a positive stand on specific issues. In spite of the dogmatism and confidence of election time, the position of the successful majority on specific issues has usually not been made very clear. Political leaders are often careful to confine themselves to generalities; for judiciously selected generalities are much more likely to win majority support than are commitments on specific issues. To advocate a protective tariff in principle is much more likely to win votes than to name the specific imports on which duties are to be imposed. In the former case, the voter thinks only of the general protection of domestic manufacture; in the latter, he may be antagonized by the mention of some import on which the imposition of duty would increase his own productive or merchandising costs. More voters will be "for labor" in general than for some law intended to advance its cause in some specific way and to some specific degree. Minorities, especially minorities which have little hope of political success, take no risk in challenging and heckling majority representatives with embarrassingly specific questions.

If minorities are adequately protected, as they are in a true democracy, they also keep alive the spirit of independence. The suppression of minorities, on the contrary, has a tendency to develop slavish conformance. The protection of minorities encourages original political thinking; their suppression discourages this. It may be true that the maintenance of a dissenting point of view is a greater test of moral and possibly physical courage in an autocracy than in a democracy. Nevertheless, since few people are heroes or can be expected to be such, the atmosphere of an autocracy is unfavorable to the development of dissenting opinions.

It is even more unfriendly to the expression of such opinions. Dissent is so foreign to the nature of autocracy that even the threat of the transformation of non-conformist ideas into action is often ruthlessly suppressed. Dogmatism and autocracy are averse to risking their fortunes in free competition with opposed points of view. They prefer to create for themselves, by liquidation and education, a perfectly safe environment in which there are no rivals and in which there is no challenge to their rightness and their authority. In autocracies, dissent therefore requires so overwhelming a sense of personal rightness and so dauntless a spirit that the fanatic is likely to be the only person hardy enough to flourish in this unfavorable environment. As for less determined and more moderate dissenters, if they do not become discouraged they are forced "underground," where through every form of illegality and deceit they seek to maintain their opposition.

It is true that the tyranny of autocracy occasionally incites unusual individuals to masterworks of dissent, and to revolutionary and epoch-making insights which stir the whole world and change the course of history. Such occurrences are extremely rare, however, and they are usually costly in point of disorganization of human relationships and other undesirable social by-products. Moreover, what mankind learns from these revolutionaries might also be learned in other ways, and at less cost to teacher and learner alike. From the standpoint of the believer in democracy, the survival of the fanatic and the provocation of the anti-social attitudes and secret and illegal stratagems of underground resistance movements are abnormal and undesirable variants of the spirit of liberty. In a true democracy, these extremes are avoided by the protection of dissenting minorities.

It cannot be denied that in a society in which there is complete freedom to differ with established authority dissent often becomes eccentric and irresponsible. In the democratic society there regularly appear "crackpot" reformers with prescriptions for the correction of all the weaknesses of democracy; self-styled prophets who have all the dogmatism and arrogance of the autocrat; ambitious leaders of non-political movements or institutions who evidently propose to substitute their private dogmatism for the principles of democracy and ultimately absorb the government into their own institution; fanatics, obviously psycho-pathological, who propose paranoiac schemes for the political salvation of mankind; and, finally, political ideologists who clearly are committed to the abolishment of democracy itself. It cannot be denied that politicians inclined to demagoguery, who are running for office or who are in urgent need of political support, occasionally adopt eccentric, extreme, and even obviously undemocratic policies. Nor can it be denied that substantial groups of citizens are occasionally misled by fanatical and foolish doctrines.

But in a democracy extremes are quickly identified. Abnormal manifestations arise in a normal setting and mark themselves as such. The unreasonable proves itself to be such in the presence of the reasonable. In the free competition of a democratic society, extremes are exposed by one another and in a sense neutralized. The deep, unshakable common sense of the people and the plain practical demands of everyday life put every theory to the test. To survive, a doctrine must work. In a democracy, a policy which has been endorsed in an election has won nothing but an opportunity to "show what it can do." The victor has only a temporary grant to prove his fitness to govern. Idols fall frequently and they fall far in a democracy. Disappointed and disillusioned voters make short work of leaders who fail them. For the citizen, to vote a fallen idol out of office is at the same time a correction of a mistake and revenge on him who originally induced the voter to make it.

The political potentialities of minorities have a sobering effect on office holders. Majority leaders will be on the lookout for sudden shifts of public opinion, for symptoms of uncertainty and for indications that the public has become slightly less bullish on majority policies and is beginning to think that possibly the party is going too far. The sounder the position of the dissenting minority, the greater the risk of embarrassment. Wise majority leaders will therefore be ready to correct extremism and, thus, if possible, to steal the thunder of the accusing minority. It is fortunate that in cases of majority extremism and arrogance, practical political considerations counsel moderation.

It is of course equally true that minorities which advocate extreme views, or views which are confused and characterless, or which try hard to be different but are hardly distinguishable from those of the majority, usually have the effect of strengthening rather than weakening the position and the confidence of the ruling majority. It may be said to be one of the useful functions of minorities in a democracy to be proved wrong. When the policies of the majority live up to pre-election promises and the dire predictions of the minority opposition fail to materialize, it is the minority which has been repudiated. If, in addition, circumstances are fortunate and events cooperate, the majority may appear to be so completely right that only the hardiest and most obstinate dissenter will hold out for a minority point of view. It is clear, of course, that the enjoyment of such unusual political prosperity may be attended with some danger to democracy; for just as too much good fortune may breed overconfidence, too much political success may breed delusions of grandeur.

In any opposition of minority to majority, the general public is more or less compelled to make a choice. Even if the claims of the conflicting parties are exaggerated and the conduct of the controversy unsettling to calm judgment, the general public will be considerably enlightened. Under favorable conditions, it will be educated to make a sensible choice. When both the rival claims are extreme and unreasonable, it may wish both parties bad luck and do what it can to further this. When there is much to be said for both sides, as is usually the case, the outsider may not only see the advisability of compromise but proceed to make an effort to bring it about. The minority-majority conflict usually results in a complete airing of the issues and an exposure of the real interests and motives which the parties to a controversy so often attempt to conceal from one another and from the public. In this case, not only the reasonableness but the inevitableness of a compromise is demonstrated. In serious conflicts, it is the outsider who first appreciates the danger to public order and security and, in extremely critical situations, to the maintenance of the democratic process itself.

All the citizens and potential citizens in a democracy are educated in democracy by the existence and activities of minority parties. Minority parties condition men to political variety, to difference of opinion, and to political conflict. In their constant presence, men become accustomed to differences and changes in political opinion as they do to differences in climate and changes in the weather. They become enlightened with respect to the complexities of social and economic problems. They learn that there is usually more than one side to a question and more than one solution to a problem. They lose their simplemindedness and develop versatility in political judgment. They become informed on the needs, interests, and desires of other people and learn that these have to be respected and taken into consideration. They lose their political naiveté and learn to adapt themselves to the give and take of political life. In the presence of minorities, the individual is in a special way educated to be a citizen.

\* \* \*

It is because of the essential role which minorities play in a democratic society that some political scientists think that minorities should always be represented in the government, and particularly in the legislative bodies. They advocate proportional representation, that is to say, representation of every political party in proportion to the number of votes cast by that party. Under this system a majority of the votes is not required in order to be elected. The "majority party" does not really win the election; it merely wins the right to have more representatives in the legislative body than any of the "minority" parties.

There is much difference of opinion on the subject of proportional representation and much has been written on the subject. Suffice it in this connection simply to note some of the effects, or alleged effects, of proportional representation on the political position and effectiveness of the minority. In general, to be "inside" the government gives the minority more political power than to be "outside." Even if it has only one representative in the law-making body, it will have an official forum from which to address the citizens. The minority representatives will be in a position to observe the "inner workings" of the government and to know exactly what the majority is doing. One well-informed, keen-witted, experienced legislator, one *official* critic and watchdog, is of more value to the cause of the minority than thousands of politically inarticulate and helpless voters. The presence of minority representatives will have a tendency to preserve the equilibrium in the government which is so essential in a democracy. Finally, the citizens who are members of minority parties will take a greater interest in government since their votes will not be wasted, or at least will have more importance than is the case if only the majority candidates can win.

Critics of proportional representation are in general of the opinion that proportional representation may be justifiable in theory but that it is unworkable in practice. Even if representation is limited to minority parties that have a reasonable number of votes, it is quite possible that a dozen or more minority parties will have representatives in the legislature. The result is certain to be paralyzing confusion, if not complete chaos. There are always certain to be "splinter" parties with very small followings. In consequence, there will be no reliable "social experimentation," the results of which can be accepted as a guide for the future conduct of government. If there is to be true democratic government, the majority must not only be given the opportunity but also the power to rule. If the majority is wrong, this will be proved in due time and then it can be voted out of office and the government turned over to a new majority.

Several minority parties can of course combine and form a coalition government, as in France. Critics grant that it is possible that such a coalition government will be a sound and efficient government; but they do not think that it is likely to be. In a coalition government there are too many leaders or individuals who wish or hope to be such. Too much adjustment, too much bargaining, and too much "horsetrading" are necessary to make any kind or degree of definite positive political action possible. Such a government is always in the process of compromising; but a workable compromise is never attained. A coalition government is democratic government in suspension.

Most opponents of proportional representation consider the two-party system the ideal arrangement for a democracy. Under this system one party is certain to have a true majority, and consequently the power to put its policies into effect. It will be easy to pass positive laws. Moreover, the chance of effective enforcement will be greater than under the multi-party system since a majority of the voters will be committed to supporting the party. Politics will also be simplified for the citizens, for they will need to choose between two parties only, instead of between a collection of them. Political organizations will likewise be fewer in number, and will be more efficient and more stable.

Judicious critics of the arguments for and against proportional representation, the two-party system, and other views on these matters will be inclined to feel that there is some exaggeration on both sides; on the one hand, of the complexity of the multi-party system and, on the other hand, of the simplicity of the two-party system. There have been very effective coalition governments and very ineffective one-party governments. If the majority party does not have a substantial majority, the advantages of the two-party system are certain to

# The Role of the Minority

be greatly reduced if not entirely lost. A strong coalition of moderate minorities may govern with definiteness and efficiency. Under the multi-party system the citizens have a tendency to divide on non-political issues and to organize on the basis of religion, race, national origin, and many other differences which in themselves may be politically irrelevant or unimportant. The two-party system tends to induce people to discount and minimize their differences and thus to foster agreement. On the other hand, it has a tendency to make the citizens uncritical. They ignore so many differences that they are bound together by agreement on only the most general issues. Their political thinking becomes more and more superficial and vague. They are so consistently loyal because the objects of their loyalty are so indefinite. It may be true that in the multi-party system there is too much confusion; in the two-party system there is too little difference.

\* \* \*

However believers in democracy may disagree on these matters, none will deny that minorities are essential constituents of the democratic state and that they must be carefully protected. In the philosophy of democracy, governing is social experimentation. Democratic government is government learning how to govern. Learning presupposes freedom of inquiry and freedom of action. Learning implies acquaintance with alternative theories and with alternative courses of action. Since the ends of the citizens are different and since the citizens have different conceptions of the proper means to be employed, every citizen and every group of citizens must have the right to be heard. The democratic state represents variety in unity. It represents men combining to solve those problems of human relations which are the consequence of human differences. It is important, therefore, that a great variety of ways of solving these problems be considered. Every citizen and every group, no matter how small, has a right to devise a solution, to advocate it, and to try to win the support of fellow citizens. The political rights of minorities in a democracy are implied in and guaranteed by free elections. To deny them is to abolish the democratic process of self-correction and to leave minorities only one recourse—revolution.

Minorities not only have rights, however; they also have responsibilities. These responsibilities are, in fact, implied in the rights. Minorities in a democracy, as well as majorities, may be expected to be committed to the principles and processes of democracy. They must accept such limitations on democratic means as are dictated by the nature of democratic ends. In a democracy the function of minorities is to represent and to promote alternative political solutions to social problems *by democratic means*. The ends as well as the means of the solutions must be democratic. The justification of the existence and of the protection of minorities in a democracy rests upon their importance in contributing to the improvement of democratic government, not in their potentialities for destroying it.

PART III  THE DEMOCRATIC CITIZEN
AND THE DEMOCRATIC STATE


*TEN*

## The Primacy of the Individual

THE MACHINERY OF DEMOCRATIC GOVERNMENT IS DESIGNED TO make it possible for citizens to govern themselves. Public officials represent citizens; majorities and minorities are composed of citizens. In elections, the citizens record what interests they wish promoted and by what means. They express their opinions as *individuals* and each vote is counted as the expression of the will of the *individual*. The emphasis which democratic government places on the importance of the individual and his interests is one of the most unique characteristics of democratic government. It determines not only the relation of the individual to other individuals but also his relation to the state.

The democratic state is not a loose collection of individuals, like a mound of bricks, or an accidental and temporary confluence of individuals such as a crowd in a railway station. Nor is it a super-organized group like a goose-stepping battalion, or a "mechanical" organization like a colony of ants. A democratic society lies between the extremes of a collection of absolutely independent individuals and an institution in which the individuals have no independence at all. To be sure, neither of these extremes exists except in the imaginations of those who praise or damn them. An association of absolutely independent individuals is an abstraction. A completely totalitarian state is unrealizable, for it presupposes that human beings can be made to behave like ants in a hill or cogs in a machine.

A perfect democracy, however, is also unrealizable. In such a form of government there would be complete adjustment between all individuals. Real forms of government lie on one side or the other of this ideal state of affairs. They represent tendencies towards one extreme or the other, towards radical totalitarianism or towards radical individualism. Institutions on the totalitarian side are committed to the doctrine of the primacy of the state and those on the democratic side to the doctrine of the primacy of the individual. Strictly speaking, it is a matter of emphasis, not a matter of "either-or." Not complete realization of the ends of every individual but the greatest possible realization of the ends of all individuals is the aim of democratic government.

\* \* \*

What justification is there for this concern of democracy for individuals? The obvious and easy answer is: because the type of individuals who establish democracies insist upon this. It may be that, in the last analysis, no better reason can be found. At this stage of the discussion, however, there is an obvious objection. This answer is a statement of a fact which is deprived of all its finality by the existence of another fact, namely, that there are states in which the individuals do not insist upon this. Even in a democracy there are certain to be people who believe that the state should do the will of God and not the will of man.

Believers in democracy can find historical justification for the emphasis of democratic government upon the interests of individuals in the undeniable fact that this form of government arose as a protest against neglect and denial of the "rights" of the governed. But this is an explanation rather than a justification. For many believers in democracy, their preference for it is sufficient justification. The kind of institutions that a man favors is determined by his notion of the kind of life that he would like to live. The democratic state promises the proponent of democracy the best chance to live this kind of life and that is why he supports it. But this clearly implies that for those who wish to live a different kind of life

—who, for example, wish to be relieved of as much responsibility as possible, or whose ideal it is to serve the state or the race—democracy will have no appeal and therefore no justification for existence. This point of view provides no basis for choice of government except personal taste.

For defenders of some other forms of government this is no justification at all; they insist that a form of government must be philosophically and scientifically justifiable. Communism, for example, according to its ideological analysts, is based upon a philosophical theory of history and, in the last analysis, upon a metaphysical view of the universe. Can the advocates of democracy, on their part, adduce an interpretation of history and a metaphysical world-view in support and in defense of their commitment to the democratic state? If so, we shall have found an answer to this question: why should democracy be so much concerned about the promotion of the self-realization of the individual? Whether or not there is such a philosophy is a problem which lies beyond the scope of this study. We shall content ourselves with taking note of a limited number of facts and considerations which seem to give substantial support to the advocate of democracy. These supporting facts and considerations would remain, incidentally, even if it were not possible to construct a philosophical view of life which would dictate the acceptance of the democratic view of the state and the rejection of all others.

An impressive fact for the believer in democracy is the character and extent of the *individuality* of a human being. There is his obvious physical separateness from other individuals. To be sure, this is also observable in the case of a stone; but this does not discredit the observation in the case of a human being. Even things which have no other individuality than separateness in space have distinguishable individuality. It is true that the human individual at birth is not self-sustaining but dependent for sustenance and protection and guidance on its parents. But this underscores the fact that he later achieves this independence. His development from birth to maturity is in fact essentially characterized by an increase in independence.

A human being is also an individual in the sense that he

is an organic entity: he is a self-contained biological individual. His physical organs constitute a distinct physical and physiologic whole and are connected and cooperate and interfere only with one another. When he dies, his organs—and his only—are physically involved in this event: they alone cease functioning and eventually disintegrate. His individuality is also exemplified in his affective life. His pains and his emotions are private experiences. He can sympathize with—in the literal sense of "feeling with"—other individuals only by imagining his own pains and emotions as resident in these "other selves."

During the period of growth and maturation, the individual develops his own personality. He acquires an identity that is publicly recognized. To insist that the character of this development is largely determined by his environment is to emphasize the fact that it is an individual that is being affected by the environment. If we are thinking of the social environment it is once more the individual that is being affected by other individuals. The converse is also true, namely, that if he affects his physical or social environment, he does so as an individual. He may do it in company with other individuals, but no one of them can do his share for him. It is, therefore, perfectly correct to say that "he exerts his own particular influence."

It is, of course, in his intellectual life that his individuality is most convincingly manifested. He is not only the author of his own thoughts in the sense that it is he who *thinks* them, but he is also the beneficiary or victim of them. He can keep their goodness or badness and their promise or uselessness a complete secret from his fellows. It is he who experiences their limitations and, possibly, seeks to escape them. He experiences his greatest personal privacy and freedom in the realm of imagination. Here he may indulge himself to the point of eccentricity and, if he is not careful, go beyond the bonds of safety and sanity. If he reports his fancies to his fellows, they will mark them as *his* and use them to construct *their* notion of *his* personality. His decisions too are his own, and if in some sense they are not, it is he who knows this. He knows his impulses to be his own and feels that he is potentially their master. If there is disharmony in his mental life, he himself experiences

## The Primacy of the Individual

the disorganization and he himself is the only one who can restore peace. In spite of the accumulation of alleged evidence to the contrary, he feels that his will is free, and that he is, or can be if he wishes, a free agent. If he has doubts or is certain that he is not, he is equally certain that it is he himself who is the object of restraint.

Some opponents of democracy will not deny these facts but, having done so, will wish to know what the proponent of democracy believes that he has proved by their enumeration. The accepted response of the latter is that these facts prove that nature favors democracy and will cooperate in its maintenance. The inherent individualism of human beings in the state of nature indicates the practical way in which social organization should proceed if it is to be successful. A democratic government is closer than an autocratic one to nature because it takes advantage of a natural disposition of human beings. The democratic way is therefore in accordance with nature.

The response of the opponent of democracy to this is that the natural way is not necessarily the better way. Weeds as well as flowers grow better when they are watered; but is that any reason for watering weeds? Before his assertion can be granted any cogency in this argument, the proponent of democracy must prove that individualism deserves cultivation. For man's encouragement of nature should be selective and discriminating. The careful student of the relation of democracy to the "natural" state and disposition of the human individual will acknowledge the limitations in this approach to the problem. He will agree, to begin with, that the natural existence of something is no proof that it is good for human beings, or even useful. The fact that a human being is by nature an individual is no proof of the contention that the extent and degree of self-realization of the individual made possible in a democracy is morally good.

Yet the satisfaction of the innate demand for self-realization is in one sense in itself a good, namely, in the sense that it implies a recognition of a natural state of affairs and proposes to "cooperate" with it. If one believes that a good must be realizable, then the refusal to recognize the existence of a natural state of affairs is an evil. Folly is always an evil. It would certainly be foolish to advocate a form of government which was committed to the promotion of the realization of the impossible. To recognize the bounds of the possible, to accept them cheerfully, and to work within these bounds are conditions for the realization of the good.

The truth of this contention does not, however, advance the cause of democracy. It has already been agreed that a theory of government which proposes to realize all human ends and a theory of government which proposes to suppress all human ends are both abstractions. All forms of government undertake to recognize human ends, or ends as human beings conceive them. The great difference between them is the result of disagreement with respect to the extent and character of realization. The proponent of democracy considers his form of government to be unique because of the degree of emphasis which it lays on *self*-realization as compared with other forms of government.

The possession by the individual of a natural urge for self-realization does not therefore establish the superiority of the democratic theory of government. Nor can this natural fact be used to establish the intrinsic moral goodness of democracy and to deny it to all other forms. Any claim of the moral superiority of democracy must rest upon the moral superiority of the degree of emphasis which democracy places upon self-realization. It is this which must be justified to the proponents of forms of government which place less emphasis upon self-realization. Such forms of government may well agree with democracy in accepting the primacy of individuals and their demand for self-realization as an initial fact. For both it would then be what the philosophers call an ultimate datum. But what justification can democracy offer for coming to the conclusion that a government should provide the *greatest possible* opportunity for self-realization?

This justification is to be found in another ultimate datum, namely, the variety of the demands for self-realization. If all individuals were alike in respect to the needs, desires, and interests which they wished to have satisfied and in respect to the degree of satisfaction demanded, the problem of government would be a simple one. But such is not the case. Anyone who proposes to establish a government is therefore faced with another incontrovertible fact: the heterogeneity of the individuals and their needs and demands for self-realization. No one will claim that all can be satisfied or satisfied to the same extent. Complete self-realization for all individuals is impossible.

This second incontrovertible fact brings the proponent of any form of government face to face with this question: who is to decide which demands are to be satisfied and on what grounds? The believer in democracy insists that initially no individual or group of individuals has any more right to self-realization than any other. No individual has any predetermined or inherent right to decide whose demands shall be satisfied or to what extent. All individuals are equal in their individuality. The demands of all selves to be realized have the same right or authority to begin with.

Many individuals, however, present more than demands: they produce justifications for these demands. They have not only decided what ends they wish to realize but they have developed theories which, in their opinion, prove that these decisions are demonstrably "right." Individually and in groups they present religious dogmas, moral principles, and even metaphysical systems which, in their judgment, compel acceptance of their conclusions. Not infrequently a single individual will present an argument which establishes him as the sole and absolute authority and consequently the high priest, chief, king, or dictator over all men, who alone should have the right to determine what ends and whose ends shall be realized and to what extent. And not infrequently great masses of individuals accept his authority and applaud his decisions. Sometimes they even found an institution for the purpose of forcing all other people to submit to the dictatorship of an individual or group of individuals.

The believer in democracy thinks this is basically wrong. He insists that no individual or group has initially any right to limit the self-realization of any other individual or group, with or without the alleged support of any religious dogma, moral principle, or metaphysical system. The extent and degree of the satisfaction of needs, desires, and interests of individuals should be positively and negatively regulated by the individuals themselves. No theory or system of regulation can have any political authority until they, the individuals, accept it and in consequence confer authority upon it. The authority of regulation by government comes from those who are governed.

This suggests the answer of democracy to the second question: what principles is the enabling and regulatory institution to apply? The corporate end of a government, in the democratic philosophy, is the promotion of the greatest possible realization of the ends of the greatest number of citizens. Democracy therefore does not begin with a specific formula defining the character and extent of self-realization of one individual or institution which it proposes to impose upon all other individuals and institutions. It accepts the naturalness and inevitableness of the existence of a great variety of individuals and institutions, all of which are initially assumed to have an equal claim of self-realization. The incontrovertible fact is that all *demand* this. Democracy recognizes initially the "right" of all men to promote and protect what they value.

Another basic premise of democracy is that the only way to assure the greatest possible realization of these ends is to employ peaceful means. Force results in war and thus in destruction, and should be used only as a last resort. Since the first purpose is to give opportunity for self-realization, the first necessity is to maintain life. Life is better than death. How can death be accepted as the goal of life? War is not the goal of peace; peace is the goal of war. This is why democracy believes that physical force, and therefore wars and revolutions, should be avoided except as a last extremity.

This is why democracy is committed to adjustment, conciliation, and compromise. The democratic process assures the greatest possible amount and variety of life to all, at the expense of the least limitation. It is a basic principle of democracy that, though a rich life is better than an impoverished life, a limited life is better than no life at all. By means of representativeness and self-correction the democratic form of government works steadily at the business of providing the opportunities for a rich life and preventing unnecessary limitations of these opportunities.

\* \* \*

For most people the practical consequences of the democratic way of life are sufficient justification for democracy's concern for individuals and its respect for differences between them. Democracy encourages the development of all kinds and degrees of accomplishments. There is no ideological bias which dictates official imposition of a standard type of ability. There are special rewards for excelling, to be sure, but there is also a congenial setting for more modest attainments. Every individual is encouraged to do his unique best. In every realm of accomplishment, there is a "natural" opportunity for activity. Limitations are not artificial but the result either of the restricted capacity or interest of individuals or of the necessary social adjustments of individuals to one another. Individuals are not artificially deprived of opportunity; if they ignore it, this too is a manifestation of freedom. Variety of accomplishment, extensiveness of opportunity and reward, and competitive stimulation to excellence in all quarters and on all levels are particularly characteristic of democratic societies.

Democracy also encourages originality and experimentation. There is a tolerance, if not a positive sympathy, for the new. To be sure, in democratic society as in every society, there is an inertia resulting from well established social habits. There is also certain to be positive opposition from some quarter or another, in consequence of the tolerance of dogmatism and dissent and because of the independence and self-assertiveness of all kinds of institutions and organizations. But this variety of points of view is itself a result of the antecedent encouragement of originality and experimentation. This variety is both effect and cause. It perpetuates the spirit of individualism of which it is itself a manifestation.

The cumulative result of the encouragement of originality and experimentation is theoretical and practical wisdom. Without this wisdom, democracy could not be self-corrective and thus would lack one of its most essential and unique characteristics. For science, for morality, for religion, for government, for every phase of human life, it is essential that the individual speculate, explore, and invent, that is, realize his individual potentialities. Only then can there be hope that life for all men will be improved. Although a democratic government by no means always positively encourages self-realization in all areas—some of them necessarily and properly are none of its concern—it does excel in the practice of tolerance and non-interference and in these respects at least is hospitable to private initiative.

In such an atmosphere, eminence and leadership in all phases of life emerge normally and healthily. Individuals have an opportunity to demonstrate fitness and the community to recognize it. The individual has the necessary freedom to announce and promote publicly the ideas which he has thought out in private. No kind of society offers him a wider platform and a more independent audience. It comes to hear him of its own free will and is compelled by no public authority to applaud or condemn. He must convince, he cannot constrain them. He is free to advocate his political, social, and economic nostrums. No one forbids him to advocate what is eccentric or exotic or what is patently absurd. Within the accepted limits of public safety, which normally are very expansive, he may even present arguments for the abolishment of the freedom of which he is a special beneficiary.

His fellow men, on their part, profit greatly from this freedom of the individual to realize his potentialities, because it provides them with an opportunity to compare and to choose. The variety of ideas on every imaginable subject and concerned with every phase of life with which original and inventive individuals regale them invite contrast and stimulate criticism. The temptation to accept without understanding is reduced. Conformance based upon habit and tradition is frequently challenged. In view of the variety of institutions and organizations, each of which is to some extent an object lesson in the application of the beliefs it represents, there is a wealth of experimental evidence to guide the individual in choosing that way of life which he thinks the better or the best. Thus informed, he can choose his leaders for his own reasons, knowing what they and their rivals propose to do about his needs, desires, and interests. If a mistake is made, there are many enlightening forces to insure early correction.

Another consequence of great ultimate benefit to society is the necessity for adjustment of the individual to other individuals. The encouragement of individuals to develop their capacities to the limit necessarily results in the intensification of differences between them. To reduce friction and to maintain balance and orderliness in the face of so much difference in interest and accomplishment require mutual accommodation. Individuals come to appreciate one another's talents and to make use of them. In consequence, they develop a sense of mutual dependence and mutual respect. They develop a neutral but friendly attitude to accomplishments in which they have no interest and learn to look with tolerance even upon that of which they disapprove. They not only become accustomed to variety but come to value it as a source of great interest and enrichment of life and thus as a mark of a high order of civilization. This variety points up for them the problem of democratic society and particularly of a democratic form of government, namely, the establishment of social order and continuity (unity) together with the conservation of valuable human differences (variety).

A democratic society has certain positive effects upon the individual of a more private and personal nature, though, to be sure, society is the indirect beneficiary of them. Because of the enjoyment of so much freedom in the realization of his personality, the citizen escapes the unhealthy effects of enforced standardization and excessive official restriction which are the daily lot of the individual in a totalitarian or autocratic society. The constraints of his social environment are not so extreme as to produce the experiences and consequences of frustration and repression. His environment is not so standardized as to be stagnating. On the contrary, it is favorable to the assertion and manifestation of his individuality, and it will in consequence enhance his sense of being a *person*. Self-respect and sense of responsibility are developed by his participation as a citizen in the characteristic political activities of a democracy. All this is certain to add to the pleasure of living. For the sense of freedom, the experience of realizing one's capacities, the opportunity for accomplishment and reward, and, above all, the feeling of being a respected, responsible person who has his own role to play in the company of his fellows are deep and lasting sources of satisfaction.

\* \* \*

The absence of these benefits and the presence of corresponding shortcomings in autocratic and totalitarian states are for the most part the consequences of the doctrine that the state rather than the individual is primary. The assumption that the individual exists for the sake of the state results in a denial of what in a democracy are accepted as the rights of the individual. To be sure, it is not claimed by the supporter of democracy that the rights of the individual in an autocracy are completely suppressed; only that they are unnecessarily and unjustifiably limited.

This limitation is a consequence of the assumption by an autocratic government that it has a monopoly on wisdom. Its enforcement of its own orthodoxy puts a stop to reflection, free inquiry, and experimentation, except within the narrow scope of its own dogmatism. It quickly brings about the stagnation of education, at least in the sense of the never-ending and ever-hopeful search for improvement and enrichment of human life. The educative process is assigned a menial task: that of teaching and learning how to apply official formulae more rigorously and how to prevent deviation "from the party line." Education actually becomes a means of insurance against self-correction. In this setting of complete conformance there is generated in the citizens a tendency to watchfulness and suspicion and an atmosphere in which freedom can live only underground.

For the individual the inevitable consequence is a paralyzing reduction of opportunity for self-realization. Moreover, there is no limit to this, because he himself has no voice in its determination. Any effort on his part to assert himself exposes him to punishment. Only agreement is rewarded. Originality is suppressed, not merely in the realm of political thought and action but in practically all areas; for the individual is "totally" the servant of the state and his whole life must be "totally" dedicated to its realization. Only those who govern have no masters, for they are responsible only to the dogmas and

# The Primacy of the Individual

theories which they themselves have devised or voluntarily accepted from their predecessors. A man who recognizes only the authority of his own beliefs is in this respect his own master.

In an autocratic state the rulers are the individuals who have all the advantages. It is not surprising that they soon become megalomaniacs. The great power which they possess nourishes their illusions. The delusion of infallibility soon transforms them into tyrants. They are victims of a political variety of the "romantic fallacy in reverse": they endow themselves with an authority which they claim originally to have discovered in the universe. As a result, they soon come to consider themselves geniuses of such surpassing greatness and universality as to be unique. When an individual develops these delusions and convinces a substantial number of his fellow men, we have the phenomenon of a Hitler or a Lenin, with the not unexpected tendencies in the citizens toward blind worship and glorification, analagous to, and no doubt, as partial compensation for, extreme manifestation of religious piety.

When a nation develops these delusions we have something very similar to German National Socialism. For the National Socialist party, the German race was the romantic genius on a national scale and in an international setting. In its international guise, the genius nation is the predestined ruler of the world. In both individual and national manifestations, those in power develop brutal indifference to the rights and feelings of the individual. For the individual is only a means to an end—and there are millions of them.

The effect of the theory and practice of totalitarianism on the personality of the ruler is thus degenerative. He has too much opportunity for self-realization. The ordinary citizen, on the contrary, has too little. In consequence, the effect on the personality of the private citizen is also degenerative. The stronger his individuality and the greater his potentialities, the more extensive the restriction and suppression to which he must be subjected. There is no opportunity for the dissenting citizen to be represented in the government; he is not even permitted to proclaim his dissent. There is no place in totalitarianism for the unbeliever and no forgiveness for the sinner. Heterodoxy is a capital crime and liquidation the only appropriate punishment. Once the citizens have been properly conditioned to standardization, conformance and obedience are certain to generate in them servility, for there will be neither desire nor opportunity for resistance.

To the believer in democracy, the self-realization of the rulers in a totalitarian state is attained at the expense of the self-realization of the citizens. In practice as well as in theory, the ends of the state are determinative of those of the individual. The democratic conception of the relation of the state and the individual has been reversed. The state has become the individual. The end of government has become the self-realization of the state. The believer of democracy will have none of this, because he believes that the citizens come first. Their self-realization, not that of the state, is the end of government. He will willingly submit to such limitations as it may be necessary to place upon his freedom and that of his fellow-citizens. But the right to determine and enforce these limitations he insists on retaining for himself or assigning to his duly elected representatives.

*ELEVEN*

# Cooperative Limitation of Freedom

INDIVIDUALS HAVE A STRONG NATURAL TENDENCY TO SATISFY their needs and interests without reference to "the good" of other individuals. The individual finds it difficult, however, to maintain his individuality in the presence of great numbers of individuals who insist on doing the same thing. The sociopolitical education of an individual, democratically conceived, might be described as the gradual transformation of an individual who tries to realize himself in isolation into one who undertakes to do much or most of this in cooperation with other individuals. Cooperative self-realization involves much cooperative limitation of private action. Democratic government is the common overall agency for effecting this.

It is important to recall that democracy has no exact formulas for regulating human relationships. Since the problem is one of balancing the interests of one individual or institution against those of another, it is often formulated in terms of an opposition of ideas: freedom and restraint, or rights and duties, or privileges and obligations. To insist that rights must be considered in relation to duties is to establish a principle, and this is certainly a necessary step. But it is by no means enough; for it does no more than to affirm a logical relationship between two ideas. The practical problem is the establishment of concrete relationships among different individuals under different circumstances, whose differences, moreover, are themselves subject to change. A formula for prescribing the desirable balance of rights and duties for a pioneer on the frontier would not be applicable to the city dweller in a large metropolis. The frontiersman has no board of health to demand observance of sanitary regulations and he has little use for one. The city dweller cannot be permitted the freedom in the use of firearms which is essential to the frontiersman. In time of war, the citizens of a country may need to be limited in the pursuit of some private ends which do not further the security of all.

The principle of balance of rights and duties is nevertheless not useless. It definitely identifies the general nature of what ought to be done, though it does not indicate the exact character of what will need to be done in every specific case. The solution of any particular case of balancing of rights and duties must be determined by the character and degree and circumstances of the *un*balance between them. The adjustment will need to be made in terms of the previously established laws which record the successes and failures which men have had in their efforts to apply the general principle in the past. In all this, the citizen must keep in mind the intent of the principle: the promotion of as many interests of as many citizens as is consonant with the maintenance of peace and security.

\* \* \*

The democratic process of self-limitation by the citizens presupposes the existence of a reasonably intelligent and well-intentioned citizenry. This in turn presupposes experience in democracy. It is true that democracy is almost certain to fail if suddenly imposed upon a people completely inexperienced in political self-limitation. The prompt failure of the democratic experiment in Germany after World War I and the quick degeneration of the Chinese attempt at democracy are cases in point. Men cannot learn to govern themselves overnight. They can only learn by long and costly experience. The lessons which men have learned explain why the democratic citizen is willing and able to think—and to vote—with the public good in view. Some of these lessons are simple but basic. In the life of the democratic citizen, they function as general rules of conduct. They constitute the common-sense of cooperative self-limitation.

In every stage of civilization men early in life learn to accept radical limitations of personal liberties when cooperative effort is necessary to protect against danger. To be sure, if they think that they can escape catastrophe by individual action, some are likely to insist on helping themselves. They may persist in this, in consequence of ignorance, perversity, or mental unbalance, even though they are thereby encompassing their own destruction. For most men, however, self-preservation is a compelling motive for submission to curtailment of individual liberty. A normal human being prefers a restricted life to no life at all, so much so that he is willing to risk his life in order to preserve it. Few men prefer death to enslavement; for as long as there is life there is hope of liberty.

Men have learned from sad experience that half a loaf is better than none. It is better to accept a limitation of profits than to be deprived of the opportunity to make any profit. It is better to accept a compromise settlement of a wage dispute than to lose—or win—by exhaustion. Even strongly organized groups have found it unwise to assume too many privileges, to be too ruthless in competition, to exhibit too much power, to be too inconsiderate of the public; in short, to be too selfish. Too much insistence on rights which are self-assumed—and therefore not rights at all—is "bad public relations," to use a currently popular term. The public is likely to be exasperated by arrogant demonstration of independence and to develop the notion that such freedom should be curtailed. In case of a controversy, the public is likely to be unfriendly to individuals and institutions which have assumed "special privileges." It will be inclined to reduce these privileges on general principles or out of sympathy for less favored and less successful competitors. The public is a potential party to every dispute. Its voting power is great and its favor important.

Individuals and institutions have also learned that the establishment of a government regulation which limits individual freedom in one respect extends it in another. When a course of action is designated as legal, the individual can act with greater security. What was only an opportunity has now become a right. If the individual's right to act is denied or challenged, he has the law on his side. Regulations prescribed by law are more likely to be observed than those established by private agreement. Since the beginnings of civilization, men have learned to appreciate the support of the law. They have learned that limitation of individual freedom in some areas is not too high a price to pay for public recognition of the right to action in other areas. In general, it is true that a restraint is exchanged for a right. The legal assignment of the right to act imposes on others the obligation to respect this right. It is comforting to know that one is acting "within one's rights," and this compensates for the knowledge that one must remain within their boundaries. It is literally true that, in a new and highly satisfying way, the law "makes men free," for it enables men to live in an atmosphere of safety and security which does not exist in the "state of nature."

Men find that limitation is not too galling if it is fairly distributed and honestly enforced. To know that the restrictions imposed upon us are also imposed upon our fellows removes one serious objection to limitation, namely, that it is discriminatory. At best, men find some gregarious pleasure in cooperating in the acceptance of limitations; at worst, they experience the truth of the adage that misery loves company. Moreover, it requires but little thought to bring a recalcitrant individual with reasonable intelligence to a realization of the implications of his attitude. To refuse to accept limitation is to provide others with a good reason for doing likewise. General refusal to accept limitations on freedom has as an inevitable consequence disorder and confusion. It creates an atmosphere of insecurity, in which neither work nor play can be enjoyed to the full. Even with carefully devised traffic rules, for example, automobile driving requires watchfulness and care; it does not require much intelligence to realize what would happen in this area if all limitations on freedom of action were removed. The imposition of laws not only brings order out of confusion but makes dangerous and irresponsible behavior illegal. Men have learned that order in life is protective and that it is an indispensable quality of a favorable external environment. Limitation which at first seems to be destructive of liberty soon comes to be valued as constructive: in exchange for reduction of opportunity, it offers greater order, safety, and security.

Limitation results in inner experiences which most men have found to be a source of great personal satisfaction. Whether man's liking for cooperative action is a native human trait or has been acquired, it is certain that he finds pleasure in acting in concert with his fellows. This seems to be the case even when his individual freedom of action is for the time being reduced to a minimum. Men find satisfaction in group action even when this is so restricted and uniform as to be nearly mechanical. Calisthenics, military drill, vocal and instrumental ensembles are important sources of pleasure, even though individual action has been made to conform to a rigorous pattern. The whole purpose of action is to conform and at all costs to avoid action which spoils the "mass effect." Men have learned that these activities permit the realization of ends which can be attained in no other way. These activities are object lessons in the possibilities and satisfactions of limitations. They teach him the positive values of cooperative action.

\* \* \*

These experiences predispose the citizens in a general way to limitations. The rules of guidance which develop out of experience are so general, however, that their effectiveness is limited. They do not give assurance that men will not disagree with respect to their specific applications. Practically all citizens of a democracy are agreed that some limitation on the possession and enjoyment of private wealth by taxation is essential to the public welfare. The most familiar and best established purpose of taxation is the support of the government. Virtually all men approve this purpose in principle. Their opinions differ greatly in respect to the specific objects for which the income of the government should be used, however. To tax citizens in order to provide police protection, to enforce the law, to promote public health, and to conduct wars, are examples of purposes of which practically all men approve. To be sure, even in the case of these obviously good objects the degree and extent of approval are likely to be closely related to local patriotism, local pride, and local self-interest. It might be affirmed as a principle that the more remote the benefits, the more reluctant the approval. Thus it is not easy to interest the citizens of a democracy financially in a future utopia or a political milennium. In the face of a concrete threat to banish democratic institutions from the earth, however, many a local patriot is transformed into a world citizen. He readily expands his conception of the function of his government and consequently of the purpose of his tax dollar.

The attitude of the citizen to financial support of the government becomes skeptical or definitely unfriendly when the promised benefits are uncertain or when it is not clear to him just how the government can effect these benefits. Given concrete evidence, it is possible to convince him, but he demands a lot of proof. When this is lacking or unconvincing, he is likely to view the enterprise as a "noble experiment" and oppose it on the basis of "common-sense." There is a more serious source of disapproval of limitations on individual freedom, however, which is not in the first place concerned with the presence or absence of concrete benefits. The citizen is sometimes opposed to the limitation "on principle." He is not interested in proof or disproof of benefits because he considers the project undemocratic in the first place. Since he is flatly opposed to the limitation in theory, he will not even permit the experiment. His specific reason—and it is a traditionally democratic one of great vitality—is that the proposed activity is not the proper responsibility of government but of private citizens and institutions. He considers that what is projected is an invasion of the privacy of the citizens.

This general characterization identifies the political area in which there has recently been violent disagreement and serious political conflict among supporters of democracy. A few examples will serve more clearly to identify the issues involved. In the United States of America, there has been strong opposition to public expenditures in support of the underprivileged. On the part of the opposition, there has been the feeling, somewhat cold-blooded and not always openly avowed, that poverty is the result of neglect of opportunity, of laziness, shiftlessness, and incompetence, in short, of private weaknesses. From this fact the conclusion is drawn that the guilty should suffer the consequences of their guilt. To allow the government to neutralize the consequences is to permit it to destroy the moral effect. Such a policy would result in the degeneration of a constantly greater and greater proportion of the citizens. As for innocent victims, their care is the business of private and public philanthropy, not of the government. State philanthropy is undemocratic in principle.

Proponents claim that experience has proved that the existence of the underprivileged is a handicap if not a positive danger to the public welfare and that it is therefore good democracy to assign to the government not only the responsibility for relieving such distress but the duty of correcting conditions which cause or contribute to its occurrence. Public concern about economic malconditions is essential to the public welfare. Old age pensions and unemployment insurance are literally "social security" programs and they are genuinely democratic means of cooperative self-realization.

In the opinion of some of the proponents of these programs, the government should go much further. They propose an overall limitation by taxation of private income, and thus in the long run of private wealth, for the purpose of creating gradually a social and economic environment in which there will be a more equal distribution of opportunity for individual self-realization. The feeling is that in most contemporary democracies some men have too much opportunity for self-realization and others have too little. This is a basic social evil which cannot be corrected by philanthropy; it requires a reorganization of society. A genuine democracy has for its principal purpose the equal distribution of opportunity. The first and most essential condition for this is the equable distribution of wealth. Extreme supporters of this doctrine of equal opportunity go so far as to insist that this can only be effected by government ownership of the sources of wealth. Nothing short of the imposition of this type and degree of limitation of private opportunities for self-realization on all citizens can make possible the attainment of the democratic ideal of the greatest possible realization of the ends of all the citizens.

To the opposition, the idea of distributing wealth by law seems as ridiculous as that of distributing intelligence or artistic skill by this means. It is an artificial attempt to destroy natural differences and inequalities among men. Even if the latter were practicable, it would be morally wrong because it would discourage initiative, diligence, and responsibility, and neutralize the deserved consequences of their opposites. Other opponents argue that if government ownership of all the means of production were established, all citizens would become the employees of the state. As a consequence of the tremendous increase in the power of the government, men would be well on the way to becoming its hirelings and even its slaves. Democratic society would soon be transformed into the totalitarian state.

Opponents are emphatic in maintaining that these radical measures directly violate both the spirit and the letter of the Declaration of Independence and the Constitution. It is not the purpose of democracy to make men equal in the sense of standardization; on the contrary, its purpose is to make it possible for men to cooperate in spite of their differences. Standardization does indeed destroy inequalities, at least on paper, but on the wrong assumption that all differences are inequalities or the unjust cause of inequalities. Moreover, what ground is there for assuming that all inequalities are wrong and should be abolished? Is there any more reason for considering unusual ability to make money unnatural or undemocratic or immoral than unusual ability to play the piano? And why should the natural and usefully regulatory relation between unusual accomplishment and unusual reward be condemned and abolished? It seems to opponents of these radical measures that the proponents wish to move our form of government too far over the midpoint in the direction of autocracy and totalitarianism.

Some of the proponents of the measures have little interest in appeals to the Constitution or to political philosophies. Their approach is strictly practical and directly related to the problems of the day. It is their conviction that existing economic malconditions and the conflicts arising from them leave sensible men no choice but to support these radical measures. By no other means can economic revolution be avoided. It may be that the old way of life is to be preferred and that these limitations on individual freedom are to be regretted. But regret will not cure the economic unbalances of the day, and, what is more to the point, it will not appease those who suffer from them. The majority of the citizens are demanding a more equal distribution of opportunity, and the quick practical way to this, in their opinion, is by means of equal distribution of wealth.

\* \* \*

Thoughtful participants in the controversy, of both persuasions, will agree with those who are confused or doubtful that there is urgent need of unbiased study of these policies. Unless the controversy is to be decided by the pressure of circumstances and thus, from the point of view of human intelligence and will, by default, it will be necessary to determine what the issues are, what political choices are involved, and what the practical consequences of the adoption or rejection of the proposed policies are likely to be. Political name-calling and witch-hunting, even if only for professional political purposes, obscure the issues and confuse the voters. Not only theoretical understanding but practical wisdom and moral integrity are needed.

It goes without saying that in the case of these controversial radical policies it should be determined in what respects they deviate from past choices, decisions, and commitments as recorded in the law. Are they merely further developments of principles previously adopted, are they minor modifications, or do they in fact represent nullification and repudiation of these principles? The answer to these questions will determine whether or not the new policies represent a radical or only a minor departure from established democratic practice. If the former, it will be necessary to examine the proposals in the light of democratic theory and practice. This inquiry will involve evaluating them as possible means to the realization of the essential purpose of democratic government. Will these new measures promote the greatest possible realization of the ends of the greatest possible number of citizens?

It will not be easy to find convincing answers to these questions. And even if answers are found, they will not be acceptable to some of the parties to the controversy. In controversies of this kind people make assumptions which if maintained are likely to make a reasonable solution impossible. There are those, for example, who assume that the Constitution of the United States makes absolutely clear what is and what is not democratic, or as they often prefer to say, what is and what is not "American." Extremists of this persuasion also assume that it is undemocratic to make any change in the Constitution. It is difficult if not impossible to demonstrate that the Constitution of the United States, with or without interpretative decisions, is so specific with respect to the substantive principles of democracy as to justify any categorical condemnation or approval of any proposed policy. The situation is different, as we shall point out later, with respect to the democratic way of settling a controversy over such substantive principles.

An appeal to the "spirit" of democracy is also not very helpful. Since the proponents of radical measures usually maintain that their proposals are definitely in the spirit of democracy, an appeal by either party to this spirit is little more than a restatement of the issue. Believers in democracy are clear as to the general purpose of democratic government, namely, the cooperative promotion of private human ends by democratic processes. This is the "spirit" of the Constitution. The authors of the Constitution could not have been clear, however, with respect to the extent to which—or the means by which—this was to be accomplished. This would have required superhuman intelligence as well as the gift of prophecy. No groups of citizens in a democracy can have—or should presume to have—such qualifications. Among the rights native to democracy is the right to have one's own convictions as to the way in which the purpose of democracy should be realized. But the correlative of this right is the obligation to grant this same right to others. There has been no complete revelation of the ways and means necessary to the realization of the democratic way of life. Constitution worship easily becomes idolatry and is a source of danger to the efficient and peaceful practice of democracy. The assumption of infallibility and the claim to perfection are native to autocracy, not to democracy.

In evaluating radical policies, citizens should be particularly on their guard against extremism. If the issues in a controversy are serious and sharply drawn, the contestants have a natural tendency to exaggerate the differences between them. Boswell reports that "after the death of a violent Whig with whom he used to contend with great eagerness, he (Dr. Johnson) felt his Toryism much abated." In consequence of mutual exaggeration, opponents drive one another to greater and greater extremes, until finally the anxious citizen feels as if he is faced with a choice between black and white. Thus in the controversy over radical economic policies, each side will claim that its position is absolutely democratic and that of its opponents absolutely undemocratic; that its position is wholly constitutional and that of its opponents wholly unconstitutional; that its position is a preventative of communism and that of its opponents a surrender to it. The unsuspecting citizen will in consequence conclude that he must be wholly in favor of one side and wholly opposed to the other. It will not occur to him that there may be something in favor of both sides and that practical wisdom may lie somewhere between the two extremes.

The political acceptability of any proposed public policy of limitation of private rights must in the last analysis be determined on the basis of its practical consequences. These consequences will either be favorable or unfavorable to the satisfaction of the needs, desires, and interests of the citizen. The effects of such measures on his life as an individual will be direct or indirect. With respect to any particular measure, he must determine how this will affect his individual freedom to realize his ends. If a specific measure promises to curtail his freedom, he must decide whether this is compensated for by more freedom in another area, by greater security, by a gain in opportunity for others; that is to say, by some private or public good. In the case of proposed government ownership of heavy industry, for example, he will need to find the answers to several questions. What effect will this policy have on the economic opportunities of himself and his fellow-citizens? What effect will it have, respectively, on the power of the government and on the independence of the citizens? What enduring effects will this policy have on the democratic personality of the citizens? And, finally, what effect will this policy have on the maintenance of the basic democratic aims of representativeness and self-correction? Will the country by adopting this policy be moving in the direction of chaos or tyranny?

These are difficult questions. The immediate and long-range consequences of even minor changes in public policy are not readily determined. It is useless to expect the judgments of the citizens of a democracy to be something more than human. We should not expect them to be more exact and definite than the available information on which they are supposed to be based. If there is no categorical definition of democracy in terms of principles, it cannot be categorically determined what is in principle undemocratic. If the effects of a policy cannot be exactly determined, we cannot expect a decision on that policy to be based on a knowledge of those effects. No statesman or scholar is in a position to tell believers in democracy just where the limitation of individual freedom must begin or end. We cannot at the same time have democracy and categorical certainty.

This controversy over "radical" limitations of individual freedom and the "radical" extension of the power of the government must nevertheless finally be settled in the democratic way, namely, by the free vote of the citizens. On this there can properly be no disagreement among those who believe in democracy. Whether individual freedom is or is not to be limited must be decided by those who possess this freedom. If the government is to be assigned greater control over the lives of the governed, this may be effected only by the consent of the governed. The political processes by which this consent is granted or denied must be protected at all costs. Believers in democracy may disagree on many things without endangering democracy, without being untrue to it, and without compromising their loyalty to it; but if they renounce the right to vote or deny this to others entitled to it, they renounce and deny democracy itself.

Not only must there be freedom to vote but there must be maintenance and protection of the conditions of this freedom. Discussion as well as voting must be free. There must be no intimidation and no bribery. Citizens must be free to extoll and to condemn. They must have the opportunity to decide "on the evidence." They are entitled to know exactly what changes their politicians and statesmen are proposing to bring about in democratic society. They are entitled to know what kind of life their leaders, old and new, have in mind for the citizens. They should be honestly told what changes a proposed radical measure is expected to bring about in the daily and hourly satisfaction of their needs, desires, and interests. In the area of discussion, the great political sins are concealment, misrepresentation, and dishonesty. In the area of political action, there must be no conspiracy, public or private, against the will of the citizens. There must be no attempt to by-pass constitutional procedures, no scheming by those in office to nullify the vote of the majority. In a democracy, limitation of individual freedom by government must initially be and remain self-limitation of the citizens by majority vote. Democracy requires that the future of democracy be determined in the democratic way.

*TWELVE*

## Where Freedom Ends

IF THE FUTURE OF DEMOCRACY IS TO BE DETERMINED IN THE democratic way, the citizen must be left free to change his mind. He must be just as free to change it as he was to make it up in the first place. The doctrine of "consent of the governed" implies the right to give or refuse political consent in the future. This is a permanent right of the citizens of a democracy. To deprive them of this right is to deprive them of citizenship in the democratic sense of the term. Whatever difference of opinion there may be among the citizens as to the character of cooperative limitations which are needed or desired, on one thing they must agree, namely, that no political limitations shall be imposed upon their right to determine this for themselves. Any proposal to deprive them of this right is literally subversive, that is, it is a proposal to "overturn democracy from its foundations."

Subversive political philosophies present the believer in democracy with some of his most difficult problems. Were these philosophies merely undemocratic in the sense of being different, he could exercise his vaunted democratic tolerance and grant their supporters the same rights and opportunities which he claims for himself. He could practise the policy of live and let live. The believer in a subversive philosophy does not believe in the "let live" half of the policy, however. It is the fundamental purpose of proponents of such philosophies to destroy the democratic form of government. This places democracy in a critical position. The problem becomes more critical as it becomes more practical. Does democracy grant even *this* freedom to those who live under its protection? Or is this where freedom ends?

For most Americans, the term subversive is practically synonymous with communism. It is not wise for believers in democracy to ignore other types of subversive political philosophy. Some of these are in certain respects the exact opposite of communism. The anarchist, for example, proposes a change in the direction of the abolishment of all, or of a maximum, of limitations on individual freedom. The communist, on the contrary, proposes a change in the opposite direction, namely, in the direction of a radical increase of such limitations. Totalitarian philosophies of the type of Italian Fascism and German National Socialism are also in this respect subversive. Philosophies of this character may differ with respect to the form of government which they propose to establish and in the practical means which they intend to use; but they are of one mind with respect to democracy: they propose to abolish government by and with the consent of the governed.

In the discussion which follows, communism is to be considered as an example of subversive political philosophies and its examination as a kind of trial case. The theoretical problem is to determine why the changes which the communist proposes to make in democratic government intend the destruction rather than the improvement of democracy. The practical problem is to determine to what extent, if at all, the communist should be denied the enjoyment of rights which democracy assures the individual who lives under its protection. For the present purpose, it will suffice to identify the subversive character of communism by means of a series of statements. The correctness of these statements is here taken for granted. The cautious reader may, if he likes, consider the argument to be hypothetical and as having this form: if communism is such and such, and therefore subversive, then what should be done about it?

The communist is generally assumed to be committed

to the following doctrine: the ends of government are not to be determined by all the citizens but are to be dictated by a select group of individuals who are in possession of an absolutely reliable interpretation of the ends of government as embodied in the universe and revealed in history. "The leader of the State," says Stalin, "is one party . . . which does not and may not share the leadership with other parties." *(Voprosy Leninisma:* 11th Russian edition; p. 115). Those who understand and accept this philosophy are justified in establishing and maintaining, by force if necessary, appropriately organized governments. Communism does not recognize the right of other forms of government to exist and can not agree to live and work in a democratic community of nations. The whole world must submit to communist rule or take the consequences. Dissenting individuals and minorities within the communist state must be liquidated. The citizen has the right to vote but only for orthodox communist policies and candidates. He does not have the right to free speech, free assembly and organization, and free inquiry.

It is clear that the private ends of individual communists and communist groups can not be absorbed in the corporate end of the democratic state. Communists themselves do not desire this; they insist on the substitution of the ends of the communist state for those of the democratic state. The private political ends of the communist are therefore in conflict with the corporate ends of the democratic state. What attitude should the democratic state take towards the private promotion of communist ends by the communist individual or organization? To what extent can the state manifest its characteristic democratic tolerance towards the communist?

\* \* \*

Believers in democracy are far from agreed on these matters. The disagreement involves among other things the basic difference between the notions of intent and act. For the proponent of democracy, communism as a philosophy is undoubtedly subversive in intent. It becomes subversive in fact only when communists actually undertake to overthrow a democratic government for the purpose of establishing a communist government in its place. If believers in communism did not, sooner or later, become *practicing* communists, their philosophy would never emerge from their minds or their books and would never rise above the level of speculative theory. It is only when a communist undertakes "to do something about" his beliefs that communism becomes subversive in act.

But what constitutes a subversive act? A communist can be a communist in thought, in word, and in deed. Thoughts can be outwardly manifested in words or in deeds. Words can be used to incite others to deeds. Converts are made by preaching. All kinds of means of communication—newspapers, motion pictures, radio, television—can be used to implant ideas, to suggest action, and to arouse emotions. Propaganda has for its ultimate purpose incitement to action. Thoughts, words, and deeds are causally related and seem in this respect to fade into one another. At what point does activity become subversive?

It is obvious that of the three, thought is the most private. Human beings have discovered many clues to thought, however, and have in consequence developed great skill in the anticipation of action. They have also come to attach great importance to the development of means and methods by which thought can be used as an indirect means of controlling action. Children who have been taught to "think right" are likely to "speak right" and to "act right." These assertions are borne out by the fact that those institutions, private and political, which have been most anxious to limit freedom of action have been most assiduous in their efforts to influence thought. They have sought to confine the thinking of their "subjects" to a carefully circumscribed world, hoping thereby to condition these subjects to concrete living in that world. German National Socialism and Communism are excellent examples of the effectiveness of this technique.

A democracy, on the other hand, is committed to the policy of encouraging freedom of thought. This policy is basically a consciously selected means for the promotion of the democratic ideal of the maximum realization of the personality of the individual. It is, in the second place, considered essential as a precondition for the maintenance of the self-corrective function of democracy. It is in the third place a manifestation of practical wisdom: it implies recognition of the fact that in the long run it is not possible to control thought by suppression and that efforts to do so are almost certain, sooner or later, to induce actions which are the exact opposite of those which control was intended to bring about. The character and extent of the freedom accorded to thought represent a conviction supported by a willingness to assume a calculated risk. If democracy has a fault here it is its failure to further its own cause by the use of educative techniques designed to induce clear and fair thinking about democracy.

Whereas thought is by nature private and can with little effort be kept so, it is the nature and function of speech to be public. The uses of speech are varied, and the practical effects are very different. For the purposes of this discussion it is necessary to determine the potentialities of speech to be subversive. It will be agreed by all that speech can, intentionally or unintentionally, be incitement to action. Advocacy has the initial purpose of inducing intellectual acceptance, but its ultimate purpose is usually to effect some change in the overt behavior of the convert.

Speech is also an important medium for influencing the emotions. Man's emotions are probably the most susceptible and responsive element of his personality and arouse him to his noblest as well as his basest actions. Resentment and anger, indignation and pity, selfishness and generosity, hope and fear, courage and cowardice, these are the feelings to which good and bad leaders appeal, knowing that they are for most people the mainsprings of action. The promise of what appeals to the emotions wins votes. The opponent of democracy talks about the characteristics of democracy which appeal to the "unfriendly" emotions. The positive technique of the propagandist has the opposite purpose: to arouse emotions of agreement and approval, which are constructive. If speech has such great power to influence action through the emotions, it obviously has great subversive potentialities.

In spite of all this, democracy is in principle committed to a high degree of freedom of speech. This is not due solely to the fact that it is usually easy to distinguish speech which is intended to incite to illegal action from that which is not. The fact is that even where wrong intent is clearly established it is difficult to convince many believers in democracy that freedom of speech should be curtailed. It is true that the attitude of officials and of the citizens depends upon the specific purpose of the inciting speech and to whom it is addressed. This explains, for example, the difference in degree of tolerance of the public towards inciting teaching in the grammar schools and in the universities. But behind and underneath these distinctions there lies the characteristic democratic conviction that the limitation of the freedom of speech is alien to democracy.

The explanation of this commitment of democracy to freedom of speech is to be found in part in the experience of the founders of democracy with tyrannical suppression of religious and political freedom. The democratic conception of the freedom of speech rests on something more positive than the dislike for limitation and restriction, however. It is based on the commitment of democracy to the principle of self-correction. Only when and where there is freedom to think and freedom to discuss can there be consideration of the new and a comparison of the old and the new. We cannot have this freedom to the degree that is essential without the risk of public advocacy of what is undemocratic in intent, including that which is clearly subversive of democracy. But it is better to risk hearing the bad than to fail to hear the good.

To this point of view there is much objection. It is claimed that we can have freedom of speech without freedom of advocacy of subversive doctrines. In a democracy we should have full and free discussion of any political doctrine, no matter how anti-democratic it may be, to be sure; but we do not therefore need to permit the advocacy of such doctrines. If it be argued, in refutation, that only a believer can effectively explain the practical implications of his belief, the answer is that the public welfare demands that the believer must nevertheless be forbidden to advocate what is clearly subversive.

Advocates of a more liberal interpretation of the principle of freedom of speech point out that it is not always easy to determine what principles and procedures are subversive of democracy. If we adopt the rule of suppression of subversive speech, we will have the worst kind of confusion, for all kinds of individuals and groups will be accusing one another of being subversive. We know from experience that individual citizens, pressure groups, and political parties in a democracy have a strong tendency to accuse one another of proposing, consciously or unconsciously, to destroy democracy. If we should undertake to control this situation by suppression of speech, we would soon create a state of affairs which in itself would be far more subversive of democracy than any amount of freedom of speech could possibly be. As a matter of fact, freedom of speech is itself very useful in making clear just what is and what is not subversive and why. It is essential to education. Freedom of discussion, including freedom of advocacy, makes people think critically, and this forces them to evaluate what is being advocated. Freedom of speech creates a healthy political atmosphere, an atmosphere which is natural to democracy. Freedom makes people feel free and thus generates in them the appreciation and the need for freedom. By allowing their tongues freedom, the citizens keep their minds free.

To be sure, freedom of speech involves risks. But these risks can be reduced to some degree. There are laws as well as customs which set a limit to freedom of speech. Though it may be difficult to detect the more insidious types of persuasion to subversive action, obvious incitement can be prevented or punished. There are, and should be, laws which clearly define the responsibility of the mature to the immature. No society, no matter how democratic, can permit absolute freedom; and no society actually does. As for the citizens themselves, they are, with all their weaknesses and illusions, mature human beings with a normal sense of responsibility. Assuming a reasonable degree of education, they will not be long deceived by the advocacy of what is certain to deprive them of their liberties.

Finally, there is the very important fact that those who listen to inciting speech also have freedom of speech. When men are free to advocate doctrines which are subversive in intent, other men are free to expose and condemn them. They are even free to propose that the proponents of particular subversive doctrines be deprived of their freedom to advocate them. Free and open discussion has a good effect on those who are listening. The uninformed and the undecided are, on the other hand, unfavorably impressed by attempts to prevent such discussion. Young people not only consider it unsporting but also are inclined to develop suspicions of the defensibility of the convictions of the suppressing authorities.

The practical consequences of speech cannot be easily determined. In action proper, the actor is irrevocably "committed." He has not only made a final decision but he is in the act of executing it. In view of this, it is obvious that in the case of action, the problem of freedom and its limitation is a much more serious one. In one sense, it is a much simpler one. Acts of which society disapproves are forbidden by laws and statutes. The justice or propriety of a law may be a subject for difference of opinion but not its observance. It would seem, therefore, that the solution of the problem of subversive action in a democracy ought not to present any great difficulties. Surely, any action which is designed to overthrow democracy is subversive.

The simplicity and obviousness of this solution are illusory, however, and that because they fail to make allowance for the essential nature of democracy. In an absolute monarchy it is easy to determine what is and what is not subversive. Whatever action is intended to circumvent the will of the monarch, whether the royal will has been promulgated or not, is subversive. The monarch *is* the law. He can decide in a moment whether he shall or shall not permit a particular course of action. The difficulty in the case of democracy—our own, for example—is that the Constitution and the laws and statutes based upon it do not clearly indicate what kind of action is subversive; or, what amounts to the same thing practically, the interpreters of "the law," both the people and their representatives, have different notions not only about what "the law" says but about what "the law" ought to say.

There is, in consequence, great disagreement as to what limitations should be placed on the activities of the communist. Some insist that, since he is not deprived of his citizenship on the grounds of party membership, he is entitled to the same rights as other citizens. If he has the right to vote, why should he not have the right to hold office? Supporters of this position point approvingly to democracies in which communists are by law allotted seats in the legislative assemblies in proportion to the number of communist voters. In a democracy the cast of a vote, whether it be that of an ordinary citizen or of a member of a parliament, cannot by definition be considered a subversive act. A citizen of a democracy has the right to vote for the abolishment of democracy if he cares to do so. A citizen should have the right to deprive himself of the right to continue to be ruled by the consent of the governed.

Directly opposed to these ultraliberals are those who believe that in a democracy a communist is not entitled to any political rights. Since he does not intend to uphold the Constitution but to subvert it, he is not entitled to citizenship. If he is a naturalized citizen he became so, or is now such, under false pretenses, for he now proposes to overthrow the Constitution which he then swore to uphold. A native-born citizen, likewise, forfeits his right to citizenship when he becomes a member of any party which is committed to the abolishment of our fundamental democratic institutions. If a citizen is free to vote for the abolishment of our form of government, the citizen's pledge of loyalty to the government is a farce. To claim that a citizen has the right to vote to abolish democracy is to deprive the term citizenship of all meaning.

Those who defend the political rights of the communist insist that a distinction must be made between legal and illegal attempts to change our form of government. The communist is entitled to use political means which are recognized as legal by the Constitution. It is only when he uses illegal means that his actions become subversive. The Constitution does not forbid the use of the vote; it only forbids the use of force, that is, of revolution. It is the duty of the law-making and law-interpreting branches of the government to determine what constitutes "revolution." In this connection, some liberals are inclined to call attention to Lincoln's reference to "the revolutionary right to overthrow" the government and to Jefferson's statement that a revolution now and then is a good thing for democracy. How can categorical opposition to revolution be squared with the opinions of these great exponents of democracy? Let us suppose that a governing clique has quietly and secretly gained such complete control of the government that it is able to abolish democratic processes. Have the people the right to overthrow this government by revolution? Or must they simply endure it and hope for a better day?

In answer to this argument the opposition quickly calls attention to the fact that both Jefferson and Lincoln are thinking of revolution as a means to the reestablishment of democratic government, not as a means to its abolishment. Since the communist proposes to abolish democratic government, his activities are necessarily subversive of democracy, and therefore treasonable. Yes, counters the liberal, but please note that what you are doing is simply asserting the authority of *your* conception of democracy and denying any authority to that of the communist, and that therefore you are begging the question. No, says the opposition, it is not *my* conception of democracy that I am exalting to a position of authority but that of the Constitution itself. The Constitution does not merely prescribe the political means to be used in our democracy but also its ends. There is no evidence whatsover that either Lincoln or Jefferson were thinking of revolution as a means to abolishing democracy and it is therefore close to nonsense to quote them in defense of the rights of the communist.

The extreme position taken in this controversy by the opponents of communism is that the communist should be deprived of all political rights, but particularly of the right to vote. The political means provided by the Constitution are designed to establish and preserve democracy. The processes are the means to the ends to which the Constitution is committed. Anyone who repudiates these ends, forfeits the right to employ the means. By his commitment to his ideology, the communist has forfeited his political rights.

\* \* \*

It is clear from this brief survey of the variety of opinions held by the citizens of our democracy that there is not available in our democratic philosophy a specific constitutional prescription by which the citizen can be guided in the political treatment of the communist. The philosophy of democracy offers no "easiest way." There are only several different notions of the proper way. The advocates of all these proposals are agreed that the communist is subversive in thought, word, and deed, and that each of these instrumentalities represents a different kind and different degree of danger to democratic institutions. Unfortunately, the Constitution does not explicitly either grant or deny rights to communists *as communists*. This may by some be considered a serious oversight on the part of the founding fathers. But such critics should remember that, in the first place, the fathers were not faced with the problem of communism and that, in the second place, their particular concern was the establishment of limitations on the powers of government rather than on the rights of the citizens. Historically, the basic approach of democracy to government is the protection of the rights of the citizens.

It does not follow from the lack of explicitness of the Constitution on this subject that the believer in democracy has no choice but to extend to the communist all the benefits of tolerance. Nor does this follow from the nature of tolerance. If we approach the problem from this standpoint, the issue to be decided is the extent or scope of the tolerance to which the believer in democracy is committed. There are those who maintain that the logic of tolerance demands tolerance of intolerance and that, consequently, the believer in democracy is under obligation to tolerate even efforts to destroy democracy. The logic of tolerance requires that he take even the risk of the enthronement of intolerance. The communist must by virtue of our loyalty to tolerance be allowed complete freedom—short of freedom to commit crime, to be sure—to establish communism.

If this conviction rests on boundless faith in the capacity of democracy to survive even the risk of the tolerance of intolerance, it can only be characterized as foolhardy. Not many believers in democracy will wish to give the enemies of democracy all the advantage. Tolerance, like pacifism, gives the enemy the maximum of opportunity. Trusting faith of this sort is hardly of this world. If the proponent is serious in maintaining that logic requires that we must be tolerant (practically) of intolerance, it should be pointed out to him that the logical relation that he is considering is an abstract one, namely, a relationship between two ideas. In the world of reality, the relation is a real one: a believer in tolerance is confronted with someone who not only does not believe in democracy but who proposes to do everything he can to destroy it. There is a difference between tolerance of the belief in an idea and tolerance of an attempt to realize that idea in fact. The idea of tolerance, like the idea of freedom, cannot in real life be absolutely realized. If the believer in democracy genuinely believes in it, he will be willing to defend it, even with his life. He would be foolish, indeed, if he decided that, by virtue of his belief, he is estopped from preventing attempts to abolish it. Life is a problem of balancing forces, not of balancing ideas. A reasonable man will not be disturbed by the illogic—which, in the last analysis, is only specious—of preferring a limited realization of an ideal in fact to the absolute maintenance of it in theory.

This distinction suggests a third approach to the problem, the practical approach. Why should we not adapt our behavior towards the communist to practical needs? Since we cannot find sufficiently specific prescriptions in law and in logic, we might be wise in looking to the concrete situation for guidance. Since the only legitimate purpose of counteraction to communist action is the preservation of the freedom which we enjoy under a democratic government, let the character of counteraction be determined by the character of the threat to freedom. If special limitations are to be placed on the behavior of the communists in our democracy, let these limitations be proportionate to the concrete dangers which their behavior represents. Such a policy will be in accord with the basic democratic doctrine that the freedom of individuals should be limited only as actually required by the common good.

Limitations are imposed upon the freedom of some for

the practical purpose of protecting the freedom of others. Democracy is not committed to a complete program of limitations as prescribed by some absolute theoretical principle or by the vision of a preconceived and imaginary society. The balance of rights and duties which democracy seeks to establish is not determined in advance of experience but in response to it. It is not necessary to impose limitations when the danger is only theoretical. It could be argued that a theoretical danger is a potential danger and that wise men anticipate such dangers. This cannot be denied, but the force of this objection is weakened by the fact that it is very difficult to justify depriving a man of his rights in fact when the reason for this exists only in theory. Limitation of liberty is concrete; there should be concrete reasons to justify it.

It is true that this policy involves a risk and that he who advocates it should justify taking this risk. The justification is to be found in the fact that not to follow this policy involves a more serious risk. It is the purpose of democracy to permit the greatest possible degree of freedom consonant with the public good. There is no exact line of demarcation between necessary and unnecessary limitation. From the standpoint of both the theory and practice of democracy, but particularly from the standpoint of its practice, it is better to err on the side of too little than on the side of too much limitation of liberty. When there is too much limitation we are moving in the direction of autocracy and tyranny. Liberties once lost are regained only with great difficulty.

It is also true that when we have too little limitation we are moving in the direction of disorder. But from the standpoint of democracy, disorder is the lesser of two evils for several reasons. Limitations on freedom are irksome and create discontent. It is difficult to convince citizens of a democracy that it is necessary to deprive them of what they consider theirs by right and by nature. This is one serious risk which it is advisable to avoid. There is, in the second place, the fact that people are naturally inclined to be quite willing to limit the liberties of fellow citizens or fellowmen with whom they disagree. This is especially the case if the disagreement is political. Since democracy is committed to a certain degree of experimentalism in government, it is necessary that democratic government remain self-corrective. It follows that too much limitation of freedom for political reasons involves a more serious risk than too little, for it limits the area of experimentation.

\* \* \*

The policy which has been advocated above was effectively stated in principle in 1915 by Mr. Justice Holmes, in the case of *Scheneck v. United States* (249 U. S. 47, 52, 63 L. Ed. 470, 473): " . . . The character of every act depends upon the circumstances in which it is done. . . . The most stringent protection of free speech would not protect a man in falsely shouting "fire" in a theater and causing a panic. It does not even protect a man from an injunction against uttering words that may have all the effect of force. . . . The question in every case is whether the words are used in such circumstances and are of such a nature as to create a clear and present danger that they will bring about the substantive evils that Congress has a right to prevent. It is a question of proximity and degree. When a nation is at war many things that might be said in time of peace are such a hindrance to its effort that their utterance will not be endured so long as men fight, and that no court could regard them as protected by any constitutional right." This opinion recognizes that speech may have the effect of action and that he who speaks must be held responsible for the consequences of his words. But it also insists that limitations should be placed on speech only if the consequences constitute "a clear and present danger." This policy seems thoroughly in accord with the fundamental aim of government in a democracy, namely, to promote and protect the democratic way of life. It prescribes practice which can be followed in the establishment as well as in the interpretation of laws in the area of subversive activities. It is consistent with the basic democratic philosophy of law.

The many good points of this policy should commend it to every believer in democracy. It is a conservative policy, for it proposes only such limitation of freedom as is necessary for the preservation of a democratic society. It is a positive policy since limitation is conceived as a means to a constructive end, the preservation of liberty. It is a realistic policy, for it requires that there be a demonstrable danger against which democratic institutions must be protected. It implies that the government does not have the right under the Constitution to limit the freedom of the individual on theoretical grounds. Since the doctrine provides for an analysis of the concrete circumstances of each case, it will guard on the one hand against delusion by imaginary dangers and on the other hand against blindness to real dangers. It assures the observance of a high degree of honesty and integrity, for it makes it difficult to exploit real or alleged subversiveness for devious political purposes. It advocates alertness to concrete dangers but it condemns witch-hunting.

It is a just policy, for it requires concrete and not merely theoretical proof of guilt. It does not divorce subversive theory from the subversive practices which such theory proposes to promote, but it also does not identify them. Because it provides protection for the accused, in accordance with the constitutional principle of due process of law, and against legal irregularities induced by public antagonism or urged by public demand, it safeguards one of the basic democratic rights of the individual. Because it requires adaptation to concrete conditions, its practice will result in the accumulation of useful experience.

The policy also properly assumes maturity and sophistication on the part of the citizens. It assumes that those who understand propaganda will not be misled by its language; that they will readily diagnose, for example, the intent of the successive shifts in official communist terminology from "dialectical materialism" and "world revolution of the proletariat" to "militant democracy" and the "new humanism." With Santayana, they will recognize communism instead as "merciless, irrational ambition which has borrowed the language of brotherly love." The policy commends tolerance, but tolerance purified of ignorance and naiveté. It commends courage, but the courage which accompanies understanding, not the foolhardiness which attends ignorance.

The policy announced by Mr. Justice Holmes is not the easiest solution to the problem of subversiveness, to be sure. No sensitive and wise policy ever has these advantages. Categorical condemnation and wholesale punishment of all subversiveness, potential as well as real, represent a simpler and therefore more attractive solution. Under the Holmes policy there is occasion and justification for much difference of opinion. Public officials and private citizens will have different conceptions of what constitutes a clear and present danger. Even legal authorities are sure to disagree. Since official action must be adapted to existing circumstances, every case will require a careful examination of the facts and their setting, and, subsequently, an accurate measure of the danger. Neither accusers nor accused will be permitted to take refuge in generalizations. External circumstances, public opinion, the character of political leadership, the current legal philosophy of the courts, and the nature and impact of subversive activities, all these variables are likely to enter into the situation and to have their effect on the specific action taken by the courts. In this area of democratic life, as in every other, there will be disagreement, inconsistency, and confusion. But this is not an unmixed evil, for variation in opinion and practice will itself be enlightening. Where there are differences of opinion men have an opportunity to test their convictions, to sharpen the edge of their judgment, and to pool their wisdom.

These are potential advantages; there are also potential dangers. With so much room for difference, so much occasion for relativism, and so stern a demand for proof, it is likely that believers in democracy will fall out among themselves. In their anxiety to maintain their own point of view and to have their way, the alertness and combativeness which should be saved for the enemies of democracy may be expended on its friends. Although these differences may in fact be definitely related to basic differences between political parties, they should not mislead citizens of a democracy into a partisanship which would be a comfort and advantage to the common enemy. Some citizens will be tempted by the not inconsiderable safeguards required by the Holmes policy to become discouraged and relax their personal watchfulness and their efforts to combat subversiveness. Others will unjustly accept it as justification of a negative and spineless liberalism, devoid of conviction and incapable of guiding action. The citizens must neither allow themselves to be lulled into a false sense of security nor to be irritated into hasty and intemperate action. In this difficult area they must once again find the happy medium between too much and too little tolerance. They must keep their minds intent on the democratic ideal of the maintenance of the greatest possible variety consonant with the maintenance of unity. This is the "foundation" of democracy which subversive forces must not be permitted to overthrow.

PART IV   THE OUTLOOK FOR
DEMOCRACY

*THIRTEEN*

## The Democratic Virtues

Government "by the people" is obviously a complex and difficult business. To establish unity and at the same time preserve variety is difficult even for an artist who has control over his materials. In democracy, it is the materials who undertake to control themselves. It is the citizens who undertake to establish and maintain unity in spite of their differences. It is therefore the citizens who will determine how good or how bad their government will be. To be sure, the life-history of a democratic form of government is not determined wholly by the will of the citizens. External circumstances and internal and external enemies play their part in this. What happens to the character of their government is nevertheless for the most part the direct or indirect result of the decisions of the citizens, be they right or wrong, wise or foolish.

Democratic government would not be possible did not the citizens in some degree have a common political personality with certain distinctive democratic characteristics. These characteristics are the democratic virtues, upon the diligent practice of which the life of democracy is dependent. Since citizens are human beings and not machine-made products, they possess these virtues in different degrees and in different combinations. Moreover, in the case of any individual, the character and manifestation of the democratic personality are necessarily affected by the other elements of the personality. Thus the practice of the democratic virtues may be qualified or limited, for example, by the individual's religious commitments. The democratic personality is not the whole personality. For purposes of analysis, it will nevertheless be useful to abstract this personality from its real setting in concrete human beings and to describe the democratic virtues by themselves.

* * *

Foremost among the democratic virtues is the characteristic of self-respect. It deserves to be named first because the importance of the human being *as an individual* is the primary assumption of the philosophy of democracy. We have here to do with something that lies deep in the nature of the human personality and which manifests itself in many different ways and in a hundred different connections. In its instinctive and emotional form, self-respect manifests itself positively as a sense of self-importance and negatively as resentment at failure on the part of others to respect the feelings associated with it. Even a slave who does not otherwise resent his servile state feels injured by meanness and abuse. Anyone rendering service resents lack of consideration, without necessarily thereby meaning to challenge the authority or superiority of the offender. Failure to respect this feeling often hopelessly disturbs relations between human beings. Arrogance on the part of employer or labor leader is often the cause of the failure to reach agreement. In most people, possibly in all, there is no compensation for denial of self-respect. It must be recognized in kind, that is, by evidence of respect on the part of others. Offenses against this phase of the personality are used by the victims to excuse guilt, injustice, and unfairness, and to justify partisanship and uncooperativeness.

When men have thought about self-respect systematically, they have developed conceptions of it which extend far beyond the domain of feeling. Self-respect has been provided with scientific, philosophical, and religious bases. The physical separateness and organic self-sufficiency of the individual have been offered as proof of the ultimacy of his individuality. On the ground of his possession of a distinctive personality it has been argued that each individual has something unique to contribute to mankind. Every individual, therefore, has value, and this gives him moral dignity and entitles him to the respectful consideration of his fellows. Philosophers have developed ingenious systems in which they have reduced the universe to a collection of self-existent individuals, in each of which the individual, though variously conceived, has been the primary and ultimate existent. One of the most important sources of justification of self-respect is religion. The dogmas that a man is created in the image of God, that every man is endowed with capacities even if only in the form of one small talent, that every man is personally accountable to God for the use or misuse of his talents, that no man is more or less than a man, these are the foundations on which millions of Christians, for example, base their belief in the moral dignity of the individual and by means of which they justify their belief in the rights of man.

The insistence on the primary importance of the self commits the believer in democracy explicitly and implicitly to certain conceptions of his relationship to his fellowmen. It justifies his refusal to accept as necessary and predetermined any essential qualification of his social and political individuality. When he does wrong, he insists on the full protection of the law. When he needs the help of his fellowmen, he expects that charity will be tempered with consideration for his self-respect. He must refuse to accept Aristotle's contention that some men are born to be slaves. He is obliged to condemn and oppose doctrines which allow importance and value to the individual only as a "subject of the king," as an "instrument of nature," as the "bearer of the racial genius," as "a member of the proletariat," as a "servant of the state," as a "cog in the social machine." He refuses to grant that for these or any other reasons he is as a person "expendable."

Any authority which individuals or institutions may come to have over him can be justified only by the consent or agreement of individuals who, in this respect, are all born equal. Superiority must be demonstrated before it can expect to be recognized. The democratic citizen will never permit his respect for superiority or authority to develop into hero-worship. Not even the most successful and dominant public official will need to have a servant standing behind his chair periodically to whisper in his ear "Remember, thou art but human." The citizens with their free speech and free ballot will exert effective restraints on tendencies to develop delusions of grandeur and dreams of absolute power.

In the morality of democracy the insistence on a right is always associated with the recognition of an obligation. In the democratic doctrine of self-government it is implied that the governed will recognize the authority of the government which they have chosen. This suggests the democratic virtue of responsibility. Acceptance of responsibility involves more than the practice of obedience. A slave learns this and learns it perfectly. Since the essence of democratic government is free participation of the individual, he must look upon himself as a partner in this enterprise. The law should therefore be observed in a spirit of conscious and willing participation. Political responsibility, like moral responsibility, is a matter of growth in experience and wisdom, and such growth can produce wisdom only if the experience is appreciated as an adventure in cooperative self-realization.

Tolerance, another important democratic virtue, is so essential because it creates the kind of atmosphere in which alone democracy can flourish. In its most negative character it appears as indifference or good-natured endurance; in its most positive character as understanding and respect. Too much reliance cannot with safety be placed upon it in its negative form. Indifference implies lack of interest and thus offers no basis for cooperation. We do not really tolerate that to which we are indifferent; we ignore it. This attitude offers no assurance that we will continue to be tolerant should our interests suddenly become involved. Endurance, too, is essentially not tolerance. It implies that, when the circumstance or object to be endured is removed, the attitude ceases to exist. Endurance is occasional and temporary. It suggests the likelihood of transformation into resentment and opposition, for the limits of endurance are easily reached.

The complexity and variety of democratic society require tolerance in its positive character. Its first requirement is sympathetic understanding. To be tolerant in this sense is not an emergency attitude but a permanent policy. It represents an attitude assumed towards a possible good, not towards a necessary evil. The tolerant citizen is not only tolerant of differences of opinion in matters which are of strictly private concern, but he is tolerant also of convictions on matters of public policy with which he flatly disagrees. Tolerance in its positive character consciously practices the policy of live and let live. The attitude of the tolerant individual is the exact opposite of that of the fanatic who not only flatly condemns all beliefs different from his own but proposes to abolish them.

Tolerance in its positive form obviously involves the element of respect. It is manifested when individuals in the presence of a disagreement say to one another: "This is something on which honest men may differ." The mutual characteristic here revealed is respect for difference, particularly as discovered between people. Respect for difference is in the first place an essential element in respect for individuality. Where there are no distinctive individuals, there is no occasion for respect for difference. Secondly, respect for difference is democratic common sense, for it removes or weakens one of the principal causes of emotional tension and conflict. If a man respects his neigbour's religion he will not be likely to quarrel with him about it. Finally, respect for difference is a necessary condition for the realization of the second great end of democratic government, self-correction. Differences in thought and practice are potential sources of political wisdom. Differences thus deserve not merely good natured endurance but positive respect.

More is required for the attainment of this mature type of tolerance than sentiment. Mutual friendliness and goodwill may possibly be sufficient to maintain between the citizens the kind of personal relationships which are essential to democracy, but they can hardly be sufficient as a foundation for public policy. A law must be more than an expression of sentiment or a gesture of goodwill. The tolerance which is to be embodied in the law must be an expression of democratic wisdom. Such wisdom is the product of a clear understanding of those principles of democracy which require the practice of tolerance. It assumes an imagination capable of envisaging a variety of doctrines and policies and an intelligence capable of evaluating them in terms of the ends and means of democracy. This intelligence will need a high degree of objectivity in order to do justice to a variety of beliefs and demands, and a mature degree of sophistication in order to protect it against dogmatic commitments.

The notion of tolerance as it has been described above is not only an abstraction but also an idealization. Tolerance in action is some human being trying to be tolerant. The character and degree of applied tolerance differ with individuals, with the objects of tolerance, and with the circumstances. Moreover, there are limits to the practice of tolerance, limits defined by the degree of freedom which can be allowed in a democracy. Tolerance obviously cannot be extended to inefficiency, dishonesty, crime, sabotage, and treason, or any other weaknesses and evils which are corrupting and destructive of decent human relationships and of human institutions, both political and non-political. Even within the limits of freedom and in favorable circumstances, however, individuals differ greatly in respect to their belief in this virtue and their practice of it. Different people have different "allergies" which delimit their practice of tolerance. They are inconsistent in respect to the kinds of differences they tolerate. Nor are they always tolerant of the same difference to the same degree.

When differences engender conflict in spite of mutual respect, tolerance will provide strong support to another democratic virtue, the determination to seek a peaceful solution. The willingness to entertain the notion that one's opponents may be partly right, or even wholly right, inclines the mind to the acceptance of compromise. Whereas dogmatism strengthens the natural resistance of the mind to conciliation, tolerance weakens it. The resolve to reach a peaceful solution if this is at all possible does not imply the betrayal of one's convictions but only the recognition of the fact that such betrayal should also not be expected of one's opponents. Mutual realization of this engenders acknowledgment of the justice and necessity of mutual adjustment. Granted that there are times when there is nothing for it but to fight for one's convictions, commitment to the habit of seeking a peaceful solution of conflicts reduces the number of such fateful occasions to a minimum.

The consideration of conflict in a democratic society suggests an attitude or disposition which seems to be uniquely a democratic virtue. There is no better collective term for the qualities of mind and heart which are involved in this attitude than sportsmanship. During the period of controversy it manifests itself as fairness, that is, as a disposition to give each point of view consideration and each proponent of it a hearing. It implies the willingness to risk consequences of such a hearing which may be unfavorable to one's own cause. The spirit and intent of this attitude are accurately represented in such expressions as "State your case and I'll state mine," and "Let the best man win." In more sober terms it might be expressed as a willingness to give equal consideration to all the interests which are involved in a controversy and to accept this consideration as the basis for a solution. It implies that the final decision will be a cooperative one and thus will have been reached by way of the democratic process.

Since a compromise solution is the result of "give and take," it represents neither complete victory nor complete defeat for any of the parties to the controversy. Everyone loses and everyone gains something. The cheerful acceptance of partial victory and partial loss is another component of sportsmanship. Although men are by nature inclined to accept a compromise solution in the spirit of "I still think I'm right," participation in the attainment of a solution by conciliation and adjustment is educative and sobering. After tempers have cooled and disappointment has lost its edge, there may come a time when arguments are recalled and calmly reviewed and due acknowledgment made of what was just in the opponent's cause. The experience of compromising is to some extent "against nature" and therefore represents a conquest of self. As such, it conditions the mind and heart for future participation in democratic living.

There is also need of the virtue of sportsmanship when the conflict, instead of being settled by compromise, is settled by an election. In such a case the settlement frequently represents total defeat or total victory. It is true that the sense of defeat is tempered by the knowledge that there will soon be another election; and this fact helps to sustain the virtue. But for the time being, the cause is lost or won as the case may be. The good democratic citizen will be sportsmanlike in both political defeat and political victory. He will accept the former in good grace and the latter without developing delusions of grandeur.

But there is more to sportsmanship than self-respect and good manners. In a democracy, defeat and victory place special obligations upon the victors and vanquished. Since an election represents a choice by the citizens, both majority and minority must recognize the democratic significance of this choice and conduct themselves accordingly. The minority must give the majority its opportunity to try out its policies and its candidates. Policies and candidates are entitled to this by virtue of victory. Sportsmanship in the deepest and best sense of the term forbids attempts by the minority to neutralize the will of the people by sabotage of the governmental activities of the representatives of the majority. In accordance with the doctrine that democracy is self-corrective representative government, and in this sense social experimentation within certain prescribed limits, the majority must be granted the opportunity to try out its "platform." If the minority feels that the majority policies are unconstitutional or that its representatives are proceeding unconstitutionally, it should take advantage of the protective machinery provided by the constitution. Sabotage, however, prevents experimental proof of both the merit and demerit of policies and is a waste of political time and energy in a democracy. It establishes neither success nor failure; it is pure negation.

But sportsmanship is also required of the victorious majority. The views of the minority are entitled to a hearing as much as ever, and the majority must allow in full the enjoyment of the political rights which this implies. The majority on its part is obliged to recognize the opposition as legitimate. The virtue of sportsmanship involves more than scrupulous observance of the law, however. Sportsmanship is an attitude of heart as well as of mind. "To be a good sport" means more than to be willing to allow a man his rights. It implies the allowance of these rights in a generous and friendly spirit.

There is the best of reasons for this in a democracy, for, by definition, the minority is a party to the promotion of the public good.

The good democratic citizen also possesses the political virtue of practicality. Since he knows that it is the function of a democratic form of government to promote concrete satisfactions of the needs, desires, and interests of himself and his fellows, he will judge the policies of politicians and political parties in terms of their actual effects on the life and characters of the citizens. He will consider the long range as well as the short-range consequences. A sense of the practical will foster within him a healthy skepticism which will protect him against theorists and idealists as well as against crackpots and demagogues. To be practical means to remember that the purpose of government is the maintenance of certain kinds of relations between human beings and not between abstract ideas. It means to keep before the mind that these human beings live in a real world and not in an ideal one, and that this world is one of the determining causes of conflict and competition, poverty and crime, scarcity and abundance. Men are not only the willful creators but also the innocent victims of their destiny.

It is because of his practicality that the attitude of the plain citizen and of the politician towards some of the democratic virtues, for example towards tolerance, is likely to differ substantially from that of the scholar and theorist. The latter are certain to be more tolerant of undemocratic doctrines than the former. Those who spend their lives inquiring into ideas and teaching others to do so, though they are sure to be more critical in their theoretical evaluation of them, are inclined to have little fear of them. For one thing, these scholars are in the first place less interested in the practical consequences of ideas than in their theoretical significance. They do not usually project these ideas into the real world in order to determine what effect they are likely to have there. In the matter of the suppression of ideas, for example, they are concerned with what the effect of this will be in the world of ideas rather than in the world of action. Since they are by profession interested in ideas, they receive all ideas hospitably.

Their degree of tolerance is therefore initially greater than that of men who judge all ideas by their immediate practical consequences. The common citizen is inclined to ask, what will this idea do to my property, my business, my church, my political party? The professional politician wants to know what it will do to his constituents, to his power, to his influence, and to his career. The scholar wants to know what it will do to his thinking and the thinking of others.

The scholar has by training also become accustomed to association with all kinds of ideas. Evil or wrong ideas cannot harm him, for he can disapprove of them and discard them whenever he feels justified in doing so. The practical man knows that once ideas are loose in the world of action their effect and influence cannot be controlled by disapproving of them. There is considerable truth in the charge that the scholar is so tolerant of ideas because he has no active sense of their potential practical consequences. It is for this reason that he passes so readily—his critics say unsuspectingly—from the advocacy of freedom of thought to the advocacy of freedom of speech. All this helps to explain why the common citizen and the politician are so critical of theory and so insistent on the virtue of practicality.

\* \* \*

The preceding discussion of the democratic virtues is little more than a catalog of the meaning and function of individual virtues. It tempts one to suppose that nothing more is necessary to produce a good citizen than to inculcate these virtues, one after the other, and that, given proper education, we may expect to find all mature citizens of a democracy fully equipped with these virtues. The actual situation in a democratic society is by no means so favorable. The distribution of these good qualities and desirable attitudes among real people is very uneven and the practice of these virtues very irregular. To gain even a reasonably adequate understanding of the adventures of these virtues in the political life of a people would require an extended and difficult psychological-moral analysis of human personalities and their relations to one another and their environment. The three most important variables in this situation are those of any individual-group or individual-institution situation: the character of the individuals, the effects of the individuals on one another, and the interaction of the individuals and their institutions.

What finally happens in a democratic society, morally considered, is determined, first, by the moral makeup of the individual personalities. Of what virtues and vices of mind and heart is this personality constituted and how are they combined? Is the balance or unbalance of personality characteristics favorable or unfavorable to the maintenance of a democratic government? We know moreover that such a balance or unbalance is not a condition which remains constant but one which changes for the better or for the worse, no matter from what point of view it may be considered and in terms of what ideal it may be measured. Democracy encourages individuality and thus difference, and difference results in complexity. The degree of orderliness of a society and the degree of organization of an institution are to some extent directly proportionate to the degree of similarity and agreement among the members which constitute it. Democracy pays for the variety and complexity which it nourishes.

As an example of the second variable we may take note of the different effects which a vice in one individual may have on the corresponding virtue in another individual. An intolerant citizen may serve as an object lesson to one citizen and strengthen his determination to be tolerant and to extend it both in degree and scope. Another citizen, though otherwise inclined to be tolerant, is thrown off balance by an intolerant opponent and, in defense, himself becomes intolerant. It is true that "controversy equalizes wise men and fools and the fools know it." Human relationships are not simplified in a democracy; they are made more complex. It is not easy for a democratic citizen to determine to what extent he should be tolerant. "You just tell me," says the country newspaper editor in *Blanding's Way*, "how I can combine being tolerant and being militant and you can have everything I've got."

The extent to which democratic virtues are practised by the citizens is also dependent upon the quality of democracy possessed by the institution. It is no doubt true that initially certain kinds of people establish certain kinds of institutions;

but it is equally true that these institutions subsequently create certain kinds of societies and that these societies shape and form certain kinds of people, both in respect to leaders and followers. Men do not create institutions in response to their virtues but in response to their needs, desires, and interests. An institution is the occasion for the practice of appropriate virtues and thus exerts an encouraging or discouraging influence on their development. A well-organized and well-established democracy will therefore make it comparatively easy to live democratically. It creates the right kind of expectations and promotes the proper habits. Established success in democratic government encourages the practice of the democratic virtues. A good democracy is a repository of experience and an object-lesson in the democratic way of life. The more efficient the institution, the easier it will be for the democratically inclined citizen to adapt himself to it. If a government, presumably democratic, is weak in structure or unfaithful to democratic principles or inefficient in their application, its influence on the citizens will be demoralizing. They will become discouraged or cynical and be weaned away from the practice of the democratic virtues.

Good democratic citizens and a good democratic government together create an environment and an atmosphere in which the democratic spirit can live and flourish. Neither government nor citizens will be perfectly democratic, to be sure. The government will always be imperfect in some respects; it will have failures as well as successes. The citizens, on their part, will also be imperfect and incomplete democratic personalities. Democracy does not intend or expect to produce a standard citizen, as autocracy does. Difference is an accepted essential characteristic of a democratic society, including difference in the practice of its virtues. But in a living democracy there will always be enough of the essential elements to sustain the communal spirit and practice of democracy. No democracy, to be sure, can survive in the absence of a "critical amount" of these elements.

*FOURTEEN*

## The Weaknesses of Democracy

A FORM OF GOVERNMENT, LIKE A HUMAN BEING, HAS WEAKNESSES as well as virtues. Some of its weaknesses are those which are native to the citizen as a human being—the elements of original political sin, so to speak; others are acquired by citizens and government as a result of association in the business of governing. Government and citizens can have a demoralizing as well as an improving effect on one another. The list of the weaknesses which have become associated with democracy is a long one. It is also somewhat confusing, for some of the accusations contradict one another. A democratic government is like an individual who tries to be a friend to all men. It invites criticism because it proposes to please as many of the citizens as possible. No government can in practice possibly please all the citizens, or please them all the time, or to the same degree. The criticisms which are made, moreover, are frequently not of the democratic form of government as such but of particular laws or practices or of the way in which particular officials of the government are performing their duties. Some of the alleged shortcomings are accidental and temporary and can be remedied. Others are inherent limitations of the democratic form of government and are inescapable.

In the consideration of both weaknesses and virtues of a democratic government it must be remembered that assertions of their existence are not made in an intellectual or moral vacuum. An idea or an act is adjudged good or bad in the light of some standard of evaluation. When believers in democracy speak of democratic virtues and weaknesses, they are passing *democratic* moral judgments upon ideas and feelings and actions. These evaluations may well be reversed if they are made by a communist from the standpoint of *his* conception of the ends of the state. Each is interested in the development of qualities in the citizen and in the government which will promote the realization of the ends of his form of government. It is therefore essential to know in each case what these ends are. No democratic citizen can be a capable critic of the behavior of his government or of his fellow citizens unless he has a clear understanding of the principles of evaluation which may be properly and fairly applied in the analysis of democratic virtues and weaknesses.

\* \* \*

Some of the faults of which democracy is frequently accused may be subsumed under the general heading, the demoralization of the individual. One of the specific charges is that the practice of democratic government demoralizes the citizens intellectually. At its worst, it encourages ignorance; at its best, it tempts the citizens to be content with superficiality. The overwhelming majority of citizens do not have either the necessary intelligence, or the inclination, or the time and opportunity to inform themselves on the numerous and difficult issues on which they have to vote. Decisions will therefore be made by an ignorant majority. If it is argued that the voter can leave these matters to the representatives whom he elects, the question is begged: his vote for a candidate will still be based on ignorance. In consequence, the public official may well be as ignorant as the citizens who elected him.

Life in a democratic society and participation in democratic government have a tendency to make even good minds superficial, say the critics. Intelligent voting presupposes an analysis of relevant information, full comprehension of the consequences of various courses of political action, and the ability to decide which is best for the country. Even an unusually intelligent citizen does not have time or energy thus to prepare himself for voting. There are only two ways out of this difficulty: to give up the struggle and leave the decision to one's fellow-citizens and to public officials, or to be content with decisions which are known to be superficial. Few citizens can reconcile themselves to a neglect of the duty to vote. In the case of the others, the practice of making ill-considered and hasty decisions gradually dulls the intellectual conscience.

The ultimate effects of this account in part for another weakness of the citizen of a democracy: he makes little use of principles and, as a matter of fact, has little respect for them. Democracy, say the critics, not only encourages the citizen to be unprincipled but it practically requires him to be. Democracy is committed to the encouragement and protection of freedom of thought, of speech, of conscience, of the press, of public assembly, and of the vote. All this requires tolerance, and tolerance is actually a kind of negative conformance, at least in a general social sense. The results of the practice of so much conformance are indifference to the principles of others and weakening of attachment to one's own. Democracy requires the development in each citizen of a *modus vivendi* for living with principles to which he is opposed. There is consequently a "pull" on the citizen that is destructive of enduring beliefs and strong convictions. This accounts for the trend in democracy to develop leaders who are less and less men of principle and more and more opportunists who profess what is consonant with popular opinion at the moment.

Because of the general prevalence of ignorance, superficiality, and lack of basic principles, popular elections are simply mass recordings of "snap judgments," current prejudices, emotional preferences or antipathies, and sometimes, as in periods of crisis, of mass hysteria. The choice of public officials is determined for the most part by the platform appeal of personalities, by the character of the promises made, by the technique and professional skill of the candidates, and by the social and institutional connections or associations of the candidates, most of which are irrelevant or unimportant. It is often more important to have been born poor than to have been born intelligent. Sometimes religious affiliation is enough to prevent or to assure election. It is politically fatal to be born in the wrong section of the country. There have been times when it was more important for a candidate to be opposed to alcohol than to political corruption. Some politicians have promoted successful careers by advocating attitudes and actions which are clear violations of the spirit, if not of the letter of democratic government. A citizen's vote is often purely negative, representing something he is *against* rather than something he is *for*. This tendency makes him an easy victim for the demagogue whose favorite technique is to conceal his own commitments, or lack of them, by attacking those of his opponents. The citizen's own weaknesses and the professional tricks of the politicians confuse his reason, mislead his judgment, and beguile even his native common sense.

Some radical critics are convinced that this intellectual demoralization of the citizens can only result in the disintegration of the democratic state. They are of the opinion that in its last stages it will fall an easy victim to external enemies or that, as Aristotle predicted, the people will in their disgust and despair willingly surrender their rights to some impressive demagogue whose leadership seems to promise order and security. In either case, the people become victims of tyranny. Less pessimistic critics believe that a democratic state can survive this demoralization, but only at a high cost: the intellectual demoralization of the citizens will inevitably result in the glorification of the average and the enthronement of mediocrity. This survival of the mediocre is actually a natural disposition of democracy and inherent in it from the beginning. It is merely a matter of arithmetic: there are more mediocre and below-mediocre minds to begin with than there are excellent minds. Even if there were no further demoralization, the mediocre ultimately become dominant and gain control as a result of universal suffrage.

Mediocrity in power perpetuates itself by precept and example. It tends to discourage excellence, for excellence is neither recognized nor rewarded. The mediocre intelligence does not recognize intellectual superiority, or at any rate will not establish it in positions of power. It is willing to reward excellence in sports, entertainment, and in the production of goods which cater to physical comfort but it will not accept *intellectual* leadership. This explains why there is so little respect in a democracy for scholarly experts in economics, in political science, and in history. For the solution of governmental problems the overwhelming majority of citizens habitually turn to politicians who offer simple remedies, accompanied by optimistic predictions.

The low level of average intelligence helps to explain another weakness of democratic citizens according to the critics: the absence of ideological loyalties. This weakness, though closely related to indifference to principles, has a broader and deeper significance. When the public adopts some such demagogic notion as "Share the wealth!" it commits itself to a general idea which may, with charity, be considered a principle. Attachment to it is not a case of ideological loyalty, however. An ideology is a philosophy, a system of ideas founded on certain broad basic principles from which all other principles are derived by strict logical reasoning. A political ideology offers a self-consistent interpretation of all the facts and values of political life and prescribes a consistent program of political behavior. The communist ideology, for example, dictates communist policy. The democratic citizen has no comparable ideological loyalty. He loves his country and believes in his form of government; he will fight to protect his country and to support his government. But his love and willingness are not based on a conscious intellectual commitment to the philosophy of democracy. Since he has no ideology he can have no ideological enthusiasm.

Not only does democracy lack an ideology of its own but it allows its citizens to select their own ideologies. These ideologies are often in some respect or another in conflict with the doctrines and practices of democracy. In the case of religion, there is usually recognition of an authority superior to that of the government. Sometimes a religion or a religious institution imposes restrictions which prevent its communicants from performing some of their duties as citizens. Democracies are even tolerant of commitment by citizens to a political ideology which is not only opposed to a democratic form of government but which is committed to its abolishment. Instead of requiring ideological loyalty, democracy encourages competing loyalties and even tolerates conflicting loyalty, that is to say, ideological disloyalty.

A form of government which has no ideology does not provide the citizens with a point of attachment for their thoughts and feelings. Democracy not only does not exert this unifying influence but by implication actually condemns it. Since it is the professed purpose of democracy to promote the greatest possible realization of the private ends of the citizens, the individual citizen naturally conceives it to be the function of his government to promote his personal interests. The systematic and organized encouragement of self-centered individualism, of selfishness, to put it bluntly, is another great weakness of democracy. When a citizen of a democracy prepares to vote on an issue, he does not try to decide whether it will or will not promote the common good. He asks simply: what will be the effect of this particular policy, or of the election of this politician who represents it, on *me?* To be sure, if the political contest involves the interests of a social or economic class or a business organization to which he belongs, he may take a broader view of the matter and vote as his group dictates. But that is, after all, only an indirect way of voting for his own personal interests. In every case, he votes as a private individual or as a member of a private group; he does not vote as a *political* individual, that is, as a citizen, whose duty it is to promote the purposes of the government. His political philosophy is expressed by the motto: "God—and the government—helps those who help themselves."

Now it is a well-known fact that in most people needs, desires, and interests are predominantly material. The pursuit of economic ends consequently makes and keeps the citizen materialistic in thought and action. Moreover, in a democracy the satisfaction of these needs is for the most part his personal responsibility. The citizen must compete with his fellows for the economic necessities of life. It is not surprising that his attention remains focused on material ends. In a free competitive society, only the economically secure have time for ideals. As for the great mass of citizens, they have no choice in politics but to be practical, hardheaded materialists. The citizens of a democracy can not be expected to strike a "high moral tone" in their elections.

It is in these undesirable characteristics of the citizens of a democracy that the critic finds an explanation for one of the most serious weaknesses of a democratic society, chronic disunity. National disunity is the result of the absence of a general citizen-type. The communist citizen is a personification of the communist philosophy. His government has transformed him from a self-centered, asocial human being into a citizen. The general effect of a democratic form of government is to discourage such a transformation. Such controls as it exerts are intended to protect the individuality of the citizen. The motive for respect for law is the realization of private, that is, selfish ends. A democratic government fails to provide its citizens with a common, impersonal, objective ideal which all citizens understand, to which all are emotionally attached, and to the realization of which all dedicate their lives. That is why, according to its critics, a democratic form of government does not produce good *citizens*.

\* \* \*

It is equally true, say the critics, that democratic citizens do not produce a good government. The unfavorable influence of the character of the citizens on the government is the other half of the vicious circle. It is to be expected that the political and personal characteristics of party leaders and public officials will be a reflection of the characteristics of the citizens. This explains why they were the successful candidates in the first place. Since the voters are ignorant, their representatives will cater to ignorance. Politicians will do this either because they are themselves ignorant or because they think this is good politics. The much lamented "decline of representative eminence" in a democracy is the necessary consequence of lack of respect for eminence in the citizens.

Often there is no justification for personally blaming the officials whom the people have elected. An ordinary citizen is suddenly elevated to a position of tremendous responsibility for which he had no training, certainly no expert training. He may be entirely ignorant, or at least critically so, of economics or of foreign affairs for example, though the responsibilities of his office require expert knowledge of these areas. He may know how to get elected to an office and yet know nothing about the duties and problems of the office. He is merely a professional *politician*. In the case of appointive offices the situation is likely to be even more serious, for political appointments are almost certain to be made in accordance with "party discipline," as a prominent public official once expressed it. Appointments not infrequently go to substantial contributors to party funds, to personal friends, and to loyal political henchmen. They are often public rewards for private benefits. In consequence, the profit is likely to be private rather than public.

The critic sees little reason for expecting improvement in the office-holder as a result of experience in office. The assumption of public office tends to have an inflationary effect on the ego of the office-holder: he is likely to assume that because he holds the office he must by virtue of that fact have the necessary qualifications for it. This explains why the doubts and fears with which some candidates originally assume office disappear so quickly, and why humility is so rapidly transformed into arrogance. The candidate can not be blamed for beginning to think well of himself when the voters have manifested such great confidence in him. Moreover, almost any public official, once he is safely in office, will very soon begin thinking about the next election. This is to be expected. Running for office requires time and money and sometimes involves the temporary neglect of a private career. There is always the risk that political failure at a crucial time may mean the ruin of both public and private careers. Occupation of public office is for the politically-minded their only career, and it is right that it should be so. But tenure of public office in a democracy is of necessity uncertain. This uncertainty can be removed or reduced only by retaining the confidence and the favor of the electorate.

Since the voters are selfish, the politician must cater to their selfishness. The overwhelming majority of the citizens in a democracy are not going to vote against their own interests. No political candidate in his right mind is going to ignore this fact. This does not mean that his campaign promises must be personal and specific; they need only be general. He can in fact with safety beguile the voters with visions of an ideal democratic society. He need only identify this ideal state by a symbol which no one is likely to take literally, such as "two cars in every garage!" He must of course always keep in mind the fact that there will be a day of reckoning and that, on that day, he and his party will be called to account for unredeemed promises. But this too will merely strengthen him in his conviction that he must pay for political support. The purchase price is his contribution while in office to the satisfaction of the needs, desires, and interests of the voters.

Because of the preoccupation of the citizens with material interests, it is inevitable that politicians—the successful ones, that is—will sooner or later become committed to the promotion of the "welfare state." The first and foremost aim of the welfare state is the assurance of economic security to all the citizens. Even if, in response to the demands of honesty and realism, it is found necessary to reduce the objective to "economic security for the majority of the citizens" the political necessity of commitment to this aim remains. The New Deal may have been a moral ideal for some; its advocacy was a matter of practical politics. It is the most "natural" political response to the essential "nature" of the democratic citizen. The citizen recognizes the welfare state as a government after his own heart.

Because of this, say the critics, the politician will sooner or later be compelled for political reasons to promise even more and, in consequence, to become an advocate of the socialist state. Once the appetite of the citizen for public benefits is aroused it waxes stronger and stronger and soon becomes insatiable. The more the citizens want, the more the politician tries to give them. The effect is mutually demoralizing. The citizen becomes demoralized by the public officials, who go about "enforcing benefits, that soothe him out of his wits." (Robert Frost: "A Roadside Stand.") Public officials are swept along by the constantly increasing demands for public benefits which they themselves have nourished. The politicians and the citizens trade political power for economic benefits—or the promise of them. The natural affinity of these demoralizing influences constitutes one of the greatest weaknesses of democracy.

The administration of social welfare programs makes necessary the establishment of numerous bureaus and the appointment of thousands of office-holders. Bureaus create the need of more bureaus. Politicians have no objection to this, for it increases the scope of operation of the spoils system. Bureaucratic government soon becomes so complex that even experts in public administration find it difficult to achieve an adequate comprehension of it. As bureaus are multiplied, they move farther and farther from the center of control and operate more and more independently of review and appraisal by officials who are directly responsible to the voters. The officials who operate these bureaus are likely to be "theoretical experts" who have little inclination to evaluate the concrete results of their theories. They, like all public officials, are spending other people's money, and few of them are likely to be as careful with it as they are with their own. Nowhere is an efficiency expert so unpopular as in the offices of democratic government.

Complexity and lack of supervision have worse consequences than inefficiency and waste: they provide favorable opportunities for dishonesty. The prevalence of graft is acceptedly one of the weaknesses of a democracy. Since a certain type of professional politician thinks of an election as an exchange of favors between himself and his constituents, his mind is already conditioned to the exploitation of the opportunities of public office. Even the fundamentally honest public official finds it easy to cross the line which separates official privilege from illicit private profit. Then, too, there are a host of political lieutenants, campaign contributors, intimate friends, and relatives who expect to be rewarded. The weakness of the spoils system is that there are never enough spoils. It is a temptation to supplement the legitimate spoils of political office with favors granted at the expense of the public treasury. To run for office successfully is expensive, and public officials in a democracy are notoriously underpaid. Often private individuals and groups stand ready to offer relief —for a consideration. It is sometimes difficult to determine later whether generosity exceeded receptivity or the reverse.

The prevalence of graft in a democracy naturally tends to develop a tolerance for it in both public officials and citizens. Not uncommon is the cynical type of politician who considers that graft is nothing more than an unobtrusive means of meeting obligations incurred at election time and (therefore) a legitimate part of the democratic "system." The prevalence of petty graft of all sorts indicates how deficient many public officials are in integrity and self-respect. A good part of the public, though it disapproves of all graft in principle, has, as a result of repeated disillusioning experiences, come to accept a certain amount and degree of it as a necessary evil. This part of the public has lost capacity for moral indignation. To be sure, flagrant and extreme indulgence is resented and condemned and, when the opportunity comes, punished. The frequent occurrence of scandals in which almost unbelievable corruption is exposed indicates, however, how seriously the public is lacking in vigilance. The conscience of public officials is not likely to be more exacting than the public conscience. Here again the citizens and the government exert a demoralizing effect on one another.

\* \* \*

Probably the most serious weakness of a democratic government, according to the critics, is the lack of unity and continuity in its policies. This is a reflection of the absence of ideological unity in the citizens. The acceptance of lobbying as a necessary part of political process in a democracy is recognition of this fact. To effect a solution of the conflict of pressure groups by compromise is, to be sure, the only course open to public officials. Instead of deciding upon a basic policy and insisting on its application in these conflicts, the public official must try to maneuver the conflicting parties into some kind of agreement which he hopes will be effective, at least for a time. The policy is not to settle the conflict but merely to end it for the time being. This, says the critic, is a confession of political bankruptcy.

Unity in the administration of the government is obviously impossible, first, because too many conflicting interests and too many different political philosophies are represented in the government. At any moment, the government represents a mixture of loyalties. Rule by the majority party does not necessarily mean rule by a unified policy. A political party is itself constituted of groups which have conflicting interests and thus have their own notions of what the party should do while it is in power. If a political party, for example, manages to gather within its folds both labor and agriculture, the union will represent no more than a temporary pooling of political interests. The differences in basic interests will remain, because they represent differences in economic interests. In the history of our democracy, economic and social groups have shifted from one party to another, the shift being determined by the promises of the party leaders.

Even where there is a most unusual degree of unity in the majority party, there are the minority parties to prevent the adoption or administration of the majority policies. In the two party system, the situation is at its worst, for here all dissenting groups are united by their opposition to the majority. The guiding political interest of the minority party is to dislodge the majority party from power; it will therefore do everything it can to make a failure of its administration of the government. It will permit the majority to make as many mistakes as possible. The minority will trumpet even minor mistakes over the country. It will ascribe to the majority party responsibility even for crises and misfortunes for which it should not be held responsible.

In the opinion of the critics, government in a democracy must inevitably degenerate into a game of maneuvering for political power. For this reason, the promotion of disunity is a conscious motive in democratic party politics. One party will deliberately exaggerate the differences between its policies and those of a rival party in such a way that its own policies will seem to be greatly preferable. In a two-party system, sharp differentiation is normally to the advantage of both parties. If the citizen is not offered a clear alternative, he will find it difficult to choose, and this will endanger party loyalty and the existence of the party. There have been instances when the party out of power has tried to minimize the differences between its policies and those of the party in power, hoping in this way to neutralize the advantage of the majority party. The record seems to indicate that this strategy is not too successful. If a citizen wishes to change his party allegiance, he is not going to do this because the policies of the new party are the same as those of his old party.

In any democracy, but particularly in one in which the two-party system prevails, there are a large number of citizens who are "independent" voters. They are independent for various reasons: "on principle," because they are uncertain, or because they cannot bring themselves to accept wholly the policies of either party. The attitude of some of them is "A plague on both your houses." Whatever the reason for their independence, they are numerous enough to hold the balance of power. Because of their "independence," they are politically very mobile. By shifting from one party to the other they can make or break the majority party in a single election. They make the tenure in office of the majority party very uncertain. They are an important permanent cause of the chronic disunity which is characteristic of a democracy.

The causes of disunity in democratic government are necessarily also causes of the lack of continuity. In the matter of governing experience, there is likely to be little carry-over. Sometimes there is a deliberate refusal to accept the lessons of experience. If one party succeeds the other in office, politically-minded leaders usually feel that a complete change of policy is called for. They consider this the best way to demonstrate to the voters how mistaken the defeated party was in its policies. Change in policies is usually accompanied by a complete change in the policy-forming and policy-executing personnel. This is part of the demonstration of the possession of "greater wisdom." In forming new policies and in appointing new personnel, wise party leaders do not for a moment forget the next election. The voice of the voters is more important than the voice of experience. The politicians know that if "things go wrong" the voters will "throw the rascals out." If the tenure of the government were certain, there could, and no doubt would be a calm systematic study of the problem. But when there is a crisis in a democracy, say an economic depression, the politicians immediately take "emergency measures" which are not intended to cure the disease but to allay the symptoms. The purpose of such measures is to effect a political, not an economic cure. Politicians do not have convictions, they have ambitions. They know that the people want immediate results, not long-term solutions. Politicians and voters thus cooperate in the practice of opportunism and in the perpetuation of instability. Democracy is indeed experimentation in government, but it is experimentation without the wisdom and the courage to accept the lessons of experience. It is "hand-to-mouth" government.

\* \* \*

Critics of democracy are of the opinion that the lack of unity and continuity in democratic government is also the principal cause of one of the most serious "external" weaknesses of democracy, namely, the confused, erratic, and generally unpredictable character of its foreign policy. They point out several specific causes and effects. The constitutional division of power to determine foreign policy between the executive and legislative branches of the government permits a difference of opinion between them to prevent or seriously delay the adoption or execution of measures which may be essential to the safety of the nation. The difference may be genuine or merely assumed for political reasons. In either case, the creation of an impression of disunity may have the effect of a policy. Enemies are emboldened to act by manifestations of disunity, for disunity is proof of temporary or permanent weakness. Internal weaknesses are the allies of external enemies.

The foreign policy of the government at any time will be the foreign policy of the party in power. It will therefore be a partisan policy; and this in spite of the fact that the foreign policy concerns everyone in the country, that it often has nothing to do with internal politics, and that it is supposed to be directed at foreign countries and not at internal political rivals. So strong is this partisan conception—and so traditional —that even in the most critical times, many professional politicians actually object to participation of the minority party in the formulation of foreign policy. They are quite willing that the members of the minority party shall pay for a war with

## The Weaknesses of Democracy

their money and their lives, but they refuse to permit representatives of the minority to have a voice in this policy. They insist on being politically partisan in foreign policy even when opinion is non-partisan. They insist on maintaining disunity when there is only unity. Foreign policy for them is a part of domestic political strategy. The unpleasant truth is that, whether they realize it or not, they place party loyalty above loyalty to country.

In a democracy, all public officials are party choices and are selected in accordance with the standards and the political needs of the party. An ambassador to a foreign country may well have no other "qualification" for the delicate and important task of diplomatic agent than that he once made a substantial contribution to the party treasury, that he is a friend of an influential party leader, or that he is a deserving party-man who is out of a job and needs a comfortable berth. The only training which most public officials responsible for foreign relations have received is in domestic politics. Except in periods of crisis—when it may well be too late to reform—candidates for even the highest elective offices "run" on a platform concerned only, or principally, with domestic issues. Those who are elected acquire, by virtue of that fact, the right to appoint the leading figures in the foreign policy area. It is true that in the various departments of the government there is present a corps of specialists whose tenure is more or less permanent and whose knowledge and experience are available to elected and appointed officials. But these experts have no power of decision; constitutionally this is vested in the elected and appointed officials. Thus the president of the United States can overrule not only his appointee, the secretary of state, but the latter's whole expert advisory corps as well. The success of the foreign policy of such a government as ours therefore depends almost wholly upon the willingness of the highest executives of the government to seek and follow the advice of courageous, objective, patriotic, non-partisan experts.

Even if in one administration the government should succeed in establishing a far-seeing foreign policy, the following administration would have the right and the power to discard it. The fact is that in the United States there is a decision on foreign policy every four years. If important congressional elections intervene, the period may be as short as two years. Thus the continuity of the national foreign policy is always in danger of being disturbed or disrupted. It is true that in periods of great crisis—if, for example, the election occurs when the country is deeply involved in a war—only the most brazen and irresponsible professional politicians will dare to endanger the safety of the country by playing "politics as usual." But except for such times, the foreign policy of the country is certain to be an election issue. In consequence, this policy is likely to be more sensitive to domestic public opinion than to the demands of the international situation.

How, asks the critic, can we reasonably expect the milkman and the grocer, the farmer and the laborer, the housewife and the saleslady, the stenographer and the clerk, the manufacturer and the banker, to decide what should be the relation of the nation to all the other nations of the world? They know little if anything about the people of these nations and they cannot possibly have competent knowledge of the intentions and ambitions of their governments. Even the professors in our colleges and universities, which acceptedly represent the highest level of education, are expert only in their own specialties. A great mathematician is not by virtue of that fact an expert on foreign policy. No sensible human being expects an ordinary citizen to tell the mathematician how to solve his problems. Why should the mathematician be expected to vote intelligently on foreign policy? It is true that he may vote for or against a candidate without giving any consideration to his stand on foreign policy; the successful candidate on his part will nevertheless help to determine foreign policy.

The fact is that voters definitely register their opinions on foreign policy issues by means of their votes and thus empower successful candidates to put their policies into effect. The more serious the issues, the more articulate are the voters; the more articulate the voters, the more dangerous is their ignorance. Let us take as an example their motivations in voting on military preparedness. The citizens do not take a long range view of this problem; they do not decide on the future military needs of the country in the light of history but only in terms of the needs of the immediate present. And they do the latter only in times of emergency. At other times their decisions are made wholly in terms of their peacetime interests. They are oriented to living in a democracy, not to living in a world which is not a democracy. They cannot bring themselves to accept military preparedness as a permanent instrument of foreign policy. A war is for them merely a temporary interruption, and therefore preparation for it is looked upon as a temporary remedial measure, like a dose of medicine.

Even when they are at war they insist on asserting their "democratic rights." In the critical pre-war period and sometimes even in the early stages of the war, economic groups—labor, manufacturers, distributors—insist on maintaining their identity and protecting their group privileges. Labor may call a strike and manufacturers may refuse to submit to price controls. Educators, professionally intent on "building for the future," may unwittingly manifest a lack of interest in the needs of the present. Individuals as well as organized groups are inclined to insist on "democracy as usual." Only after serious defeat and in great danger do they develop a wholehearted nationalism.

Nor do they learn from their war-experiences. While they are at war they deceive themselves with romantic slogans and designate the war in which they are engaged as "A war to end war," or "A war to make the world safe for democracy." They like these slogans because they make their participation in the war seem morally justifiable. And they believe them, as is indicated by the fact that as soon as the war is won they clamor for disarmament. Between wars they are easily induced to join in movements which propose to establish universal peace. Friends of peace, with the cooperation of shrewd enemies, induce them to disarm. They demobilize, sink battleships, destroy ordnance or let it rust and deteriorate, liquidate supplies and equipment at tremendous financial sacrifice, deprive the standing military organization of financial and moral support, and, in an unbelievably short time, sink back into their original state of unpreparedness. Although more than once they have had to rearm to meet aggression, although between wars their enemies instead of disarming strain every effort to rearm twice as strongly, although they have more than once failed to outlaw war, and although history clearly proves that each time the cost of "making the world safe for democracy," is more frightful, they are still not convinced that the only secure nation is an armed nation.

It is to be expected that the politicians, and therefore their government, will reflect these unfortunate weaknesses. Those representatives who have been elected by special economic groups are not likely to forget their obligations. The adoption of measures essential to military preparedness will be delayed by practical politics. The democratic technique of compromise will be given up only in the most serious emergency. The opposition party will be on the lookout for mistakes by the government and be ready and willing to tell the voters about them. Military defeats, if properly explained, can be very useful, at the moment or later, in discrediting the government's conduct of the war. When the war is over, political capital can be made out of the post-war reactions of the voters. The voters will not forget the public official who exerted himself in "bringing the boys back home."

How can a representative of the people be expected to do otherwise, even if he knows or suspects that the nation's enemies, actual and potential, will be much pleased! A democratic government cannot rule without the consent of the governed. A democratic government cannot force preparedness on the people. Some historians and analysts of international affairs point to World War I and II as proof of the weaknesses of the foreign policies of the great democracies. They were to a considerable extent the immediate consequences of the naiveté, romantic pacifism, provincialism and isolationism, over-concentration on business and money-making, disunity and lack of discipline, and love of luxury of the democracies. The enemy saw his opportunity in the absorption of the democratic peoples in business and their acceptance of the rule of business that "The customer is always right." Do not democracies regularly permit their citizens to trade with the potential enemy, including permission to provide them, up to the last minute, with military supplies? Did not England and the United States finance the rearming of Germany after World War I and did not the United States help to arm Japan just before the second one? Both wars were the result of short-sighted foreign policies. Victory in war can hardly be considered as proof of the success of a foreign policy. A realistic and determined foreign policy would have prevented war.

The real problem, therefore, is the prevention of war. For this task, say the critics, a democracy is ill equipped because of its inherent weaknesses. A democracy can survive only in a world which is wholly democratic or in which the balance of strength is overwhelmingly in favor of existing democracies. This strength must be intellectual as well as physical. It must represent an alliance of wisdom and brute force. This alliance must be the instrument of a foreign policy which must have unity and continuity. Behind this policy there must be a nation which is able and willing to support this policy. Much as we may prefer democracy, we must have serious doubts whether in its present form, with its many weaknesses, it can survive in a world which to date has shown little interest in the democratic ideal of "live and let live."

*FIFTEEN*

# A Trial Balance

A WISE BELIEVER IN DEMOCRACY WILL WISH TO EXAMINE AND evaluate the alleged weaknesses of his chosen form of government dispassionately and objectively. This will involve two steps. It will be necessary, first, to determine the facts in the case. This being done, he will be prepared to pass one of several judgments: he may deny the justice or the merit of the criticism; he may judge it to be exaggerated in one respect or another; he may agree that the weakness is present but claim that its effects are somehow neutralized; or he may acknowledge the existence of the weakness and freely grant that there is no escape from it. Factual examination will enable him to distinguish real weaknesses from those weaknesses which exist only in the minds of ideological opponents of democracy. The facts having been established, the believer in democracy can then compare strong and weak points with those of other forms of government and take his choice.

In the case of several of the weaknesses of which democracy is accused, satisfactory factual evidence is not easily obtained. How, for example, is the investigator to prove that a social security program does or does not have the alleged demoralizing effect on the sense of responsibility of the citizen? To prove this with facts, it would be necessary to make an extended comparative study of the manifestations of responsibility by a representative number of the citizens before and after the initia-

# A Trial Balance

tion of the program. In the case of the alleged stimulation of selfishness in the democratic citizen, it must be determined if participation in democratic government does not have a counteracting effect and, instead of stimulating selfishness, does not actually train the citizen in unselfish cooperation. A particular characteristic of government or of a citizen does not exist in isolation; it is part of a complex, of an individual or social personality. To determine the effects of a form of government and the citizens upon one another requires expert and extended psychological and sociological analysis.

Final evaluation of the facts presupposes convictions with regard to the desirability or undesirability of the effects which have been discovered. This requires a clear understanding of the general conception of the good life which is presupposed and, specifically, of the ends of government which have been selected as desirable. It also involves a delicate balancing of too much against too little; it involves quantitative measurement of the effect under investigation. What follows is little more than a marshalling of some ideas which must be taken into consideration in any evaluation of the alleged strong and weak points of the democratic citizen and his government. It is a kind of trial balance, the purpose of which is to suggest the kind of data and principles of evaluation which are required for a final accounting.

\* \* \*

The student of democracy will willingly grant that the citizens of a democracy are certain to be ignorant of much that they should know. It is one of the virtues of democracy, however, that it allows for ignorance and makes generous provision for dispelling it. Democracies believe in universal education because they recognize the dangers of ignorance. Education awakens in the citizen and prospective citizen the consciousness of his ignorance. The exposure to formal and informal education conditions the citizens to evaluate expressions of opinion. The citizen who reads and hears the endless discussions of social, economic, and political issues by editorial writers, commentators, educators, popular lecturers, and politicians, cannot help but become to some degree informed on these issues. In many cases, a reasonable degree of native intelligence, not improperly called common sense, will enable him to recognize what is sound doctrine. He may not be able to absorb and digest the arguments in detail but he will sense the *thrust* of the argument; he will recognize its tendency and develop some notion of the practical consequences of the policies which are advocated. He will develop some ability to distinguish sincerity from insincerity, objectivity from prejudice, information from humbug. This is the "common-sense" of the people upon which Thomas Jefferson based his faith in democracy.

Now it is a characteristic of common sense not to be very much impressed with theories. The lack of respect for theories has its origin in the popular suspicion that theories are not practical. This suspicion is transferred to those who produce the theories, namely, the experts. It is to some extent justified by the fact that not infrequently the claims of the experts are discredited by events. Another reason why the people have so little faith in experts is the fact that the latter so often disagree. The citizens become even more skeptical of theories when experienced political leaders—practical experts, therefore —are proved wrong. Rightly or wrongly, the common man feels that experts should never be so completely wrong. When they are, the most likely explanation which occurs to him is that the judgments of both academic and "practical" experts must have been based upon theories rather than facts. This is one reason why the citizens have so little interest in principles and ideologies.

Another reason is that everyday life demands of him that he be practical, that is, responsive to the demands of a specific situation. He likes to sing about freedom and justice and to hear great men extol them on patriotic occasions. The glorification of the great principles of democracy stirs him emotionally; but when it comes to everyday living he is more concerned about the wages he earns, the prices he pays, and the taxes he has to raise. When he is faced with the necessity of voting on broad principles such as are involved in international policy, his ideas are vague and his judgment uncertain. He knows exactly what to do about such a "fact" as a Pearl Harbor but not what to do about such a policy as Western solidarity. It is only on local political issues that he feels reasonably sure of himself.

In passing judgment on the theoretical ignorance of the democratic citizen, it should not be forgotten that he is not committed in advance, as is his authoritarian counterpart, to prove a theory. Such a commitment would be likely to unfit him completely for finding practical solutions for specific conflicts between human beings. The citizen of an authoritarian state may be letter perfect in the ideology of his government; but his blind commitment to solve all problems in terms of this ideology is in the opinion of the believer in democracy actually an obstacle to the solution of problems. It is also an obstacle to the removal of ignorance. The mind of this citizen is wrapped in the "deep slumber of a decided opinion." Nothing but a revolution will awaken him. The theoretical ignorance of the citizen of a democracy is therefore preferable to the theoretical knowledge of the citizen of some non-democratic states.

Political ignorance and lack of respect for expert opinion in the average democratic citizen are also compensated for by his possession of another good quality: his moral sense. This is really another phase of common-sense, for it implies, not intellectual commitment to abstract ethical principles, but the daily practice of such homely virtues as honesty, integrity, fairness, and sympathy. His common sense tells him that no decent human relationship can be maintained without the practice of these virtues. He may not understand the philosophy of dialectical materialism, for example, but he recognizes the lies and tricks of the practicing communist and the ruthlessness and moral brutality of communist rule. He may be uncertain about the democratic orthodoxy of a public official or an administration, but he does not long fail to sense serious corruption. He may not be able to judge the economic soundness of a political policy, but he is usually able to determine whether it is for the good of the few or the many.

As for the claim that the lack of respect for expert knowledge is certain, sooner or later, to reduce the standard of intellectual interest and accomplishment in a democracy to a dead level of mediocrity, a moment's thought will reveal that the general charge cannot be sustained. If we take all the democracies together, the facts are that the standards of both achievement and appreciation have been very high in every area of human endeavor. The overwhelming majority of people may well be satisfied with a low level of accomplishment for themselves without thereby losing the capacity for recognizing exceptional attainment and the desire for rewarding it.

When it is argued that this is true enough in such realms as art, science, and technology but not true in democratic politics, the believer in democracy cannot feel quite so certain. Excellence will sustain itself in many areas even when it goes unrecognized; in politics, it must be recognized or it cannot function. The not infrequent political success of individuals of mediocre to low intellectual and moral standards should be a source of deep concern to the believer in democracy. There are, to be sure, corrective and counteracting influences: rivals and associates of superior moral and intellectual calibre; the eventual practical failure and consequent exposure of ignorance and cheapness; and the slow but sure recognition of sham and pretense by the common sense of the people. Ignorance can do much damage before it is discovered, however, and the threat of this is a constant one. The only lasting protection is to be found in a system of universal education in which there is not only concern to meet the educational needs of as many as possible but also selective encouragement of the few of superior intelligence.

\* \* \*

As for the alleged over-emphasis on self-interest by the citizens, if it is the corporate end of democratic government to promote the realization of private ends, it cannot well be wrong for citizens to be interested in their private ends. As a matter of fact, there are no ends but private ends in the last analysis. Proponents of democracy think it undemocratic for a government to develop ends of its own. Initial self-interest is therefore in itself not a weakness of the democratic citizen; what is wrong is the refusal of a citizen to recognize the interests of other citizens and to cooperate with them in the promotion of common interests and in the solution of conflicts by conciliation and adjustment. It is true that in some citizens there exists permanently a feeling of opposition to the government, as if the government were a tyrannical monarch whose interests were strictly the tyrant's own. Most citizens, however, understand that it is the government which makes the realization of the private ends of himself and his fellow-citizens possible. When the thoughtful citizen thinks of what is done with the taxes he pays, he discovers, or rediscovers, his personal ends and those of his fellow-citizen in those of the government. His self-centeredness is consequently qualified by a willingness to co-operate with the government.

Self-interest which is not enlightened by the understanding of the relation of the self to other selves is indeed a weakness in a democratic citizen. It is also a weakness if the citizen has too little self-interest. Other citizens, including public officials, are likely to take advantage of this. To insist on consideration of his interests is to insist on representativeness. It is the only defense the democratic citizen has against usurpation of power by the government. If he does not take advantage of his opportunities he may soon find himself politically powerless and socially dependent. He will then be well on the way to slavery. Self-abnegation implies a resignation of interests and rights. Politically, it amounts to abdication as a citizen; morally, to abdication as a self-respecting, self-determining individual.

\* \* \*

The charge that participation in political activities in a democratic state is morally demoralizing is a serious charge indeed. Is it true that success in politics demands compromises with truth, with conviction, with sincerity, and with honesty, and that, in consequence, both politician and citizen lose their moral sensitivity, the former as a result of habituation to the things he does, the latter as a result of habituation to the things he observes? The ultimate validity of these charges can be determined only by a careful study of the history of democracy. Since no such study is available, an evaluation of this charge on historical grounds is not now practicable. If the claim is based on theoretical grounds the critic must show that life in a democratic state must necessarily have this demoralizing effect on the citizen, or at least on enough of them to be representative. The moral effect of any government on its citizens cannot be evaluated, however, except in terms of some predetermined conception of the desirable moral personality, of acceptable moral behavior, and in the last analysis, of acceptable ethical principles. Such a definitive evaluation belongs in a systematic consideration of the ethics of democracy. The discussion of some specific charges which follows must be considered as merely a pilot study, it being understood that the conception of the desirable citizen-personality which is assumed is that which has been broadly suggested in the preceding pages.

Critics of democracy lay much stress on the alleged demoralizing effect of the political "professionalism" which democracy breeds. In a democracy, it is claimed, expertness in getting elected rather than expertness in public service is the mark of the professional. "Professionalism" is a "natural growth" in a democracy and some of the effects are certainly demoralizing. Amateur political reform is no match for efficiently organized political corruption. Good citizens sometimes become convinced of their helplessness against a political machine and resign themselves to the inescapable. Budding young statesmen lose their idealism in the arena of practical politics and begin adapting their policies to the political weather of the moment. Undesirable as such developments are, they are not as general as the critics would have us believe. They are, moreover, offset by the influence of public officials and statesmen of the finest character, by the counteracting effect of watchful lay guardians of the public welfare, and by non-professional education in the ends and means of democracy. The fear of undesirable professionalism rests to some extent on the preconceived notion that the desire to be elected is a selfish motive and that it therefore cannot be reconciled with an unselfish desire to promote the public welfare. This belief is a product of a romantic idealism which ignores the basic fact that even the noblest ideal of unselfish service must be the personal ideal of an individual if someone is to make an attempt to realize it. The people are not likely to elect a man who is not interested in being elected. Indifference, reticence, and modesty are not useful virtues in an election contest. Once having decided to "run for office," there is no point to losing the election by amateur bungling.

\* \* \*

No honest citizen will wish to deny the occurrence of cor-

*A Trial Balance* 191

ruption in the political life of a democracy and its demoralizing effect on both public officials and citizens. Even the most tolerant friends of democracy are frequently shocked by the shameless immorality of public officials and the rapacity of notorious political "bosses." Before concluding that these evils, at least in the exaggerated form in which they sometimes occur, are inescapable in a democracy, the critic will do well to take note of the difference in frequency and degree of their occurence in different democracies. He should, in respect to these abuses, compare the records of Holland, Great Britain, France, and the United States. Such a comparative study of the facts will justify the conclusion that there is nothing in the essential nature of democracy which makes it impossible to control political corruption and to hold it to a minimum.

The determination as to whether or not there is in the government or the citizens of a democracy a native disposition to political graft and corruption is another matter. In any attempt to explain moral behavior of large organized masses of people two factors must be taken into consideration: the ethical standards of the social group and the physical and institutional environment. It is easy to be good in an environment in which there is little opportunity to be bad. Character and opportunity are two variables which cooperatively determine the moral behavior of the individual and of the group. The more external restraints there are, the less need there is for individual decision. The more freedom the individual has, the more need there is of self-control.

In an authoritarian society the citizen is provided with a ready-made behavior program and he needs only to follow that program to be "good." To be orthodox is to be moral. In a democracy the citizen is much more free to make his own decisions. He has far more opportunity to promote his own personal interest. In a democracy there is extensive opportunity for the exchange of political favors. The intimacy of political relations between politicians and voters in such small units as the township and the ward tends to encourage transactions which are customary between close friends and members of families. Habits established in this way are carried over into larger political areas. Under the pressure of personal friends and political associates, public officials and private citizens cross the somewhat vague line which separates friendly aid from illegal favor and jointly betray private morality and public trust. The existence of general suffrage, the importance of the individual, the wide distribution of power, the diffusion of responsibility, the complexity of government, and the lack of supervision, these are the characteristics of democratic government which undeniably are favorable to the occurrence of graft and corruption.

There are, however, qualifying facts and counteracting influences which are equally characteristic of democracy. As a general rule, the incidence of graft and corruption is low compared with the incidence of responsible and honest behavior. When and where dishonesty does occur it is usually petty in nature. The failure of the citizens to become excited about minor public immorality does not necessarily indicate cynicism; it may be a realistic conviction that it is wholly impractical to attempt to eliminate or prevent it. The political history of the United States indicates that serious political corruption arouses the citizens to vigorous remedial action. Honest public officials keep a watchful eye on public administration. Rival politicians and political parties are on the alert to detect illegal official conduct and are not unwilling to foster suspicions of this. Newspapers and journals, even those not particularly public spirited, are interested in the misbehavior of public officials as news. The much criticized columnists have been sources of information, as well as of gossip, about dishonest transactions between public officials and private citizens. Public spirited leaders call the attention of the public to laxity and corruption in the administration of public business.

The extent and effectiveness of all this watchfulness and criticism depend in the last analysis upon the moral sense of the people, to be sure. This is the ultimate counteracting force which offsets the influence of predisposing circumstances and prevents the demoralization of democratic citizens and their institutions or contains it within safe limits. If there is no practice of the homely virtues in the people, the state will indeed perish. The moral direction of a democratic government will in large part be determined by the character and effectiveness of non-political institutions and particularly of the agencies which are responsible for the moral education of the young: the family, the church, and the school. Because all citizens cast votes, the moral education and training of all citizens is the ultimate determinant of the moral personality of the state.

\* \* \*

Another alleged cause of demoralization of the citizens by democratic government is the supposedly inherent tendency of such a government to become paternalistic. Paternalism, which is conceived as the transfer of responsibility from the individual to the state, is asserted to be the cause of a change in the private and public personality of the citizen and, as an ultimate necessary consequence, of a change in the character of the government. The "degradation" of democracy, it is claimed, proceeds from social security legislation, through the welfare state, to socialism, and finally to totalitarianism. The debate over all this is confused and heated. It is confused because the disputants not only disagree on the supposed effects but also on the meaning of such terms as the welfare state. It is heated principally because some disputants consider the predicted transformation of the state desirable and others consider it undesirable. Many infer the character and occurrence of the alleged effects from a preconceived notion of the form of government into which they fear, or hope, that democracy will be transformed. The discussion presents a mixture of wishful thinking, political propaganda, and conscientious analysis. Although the future alone can establish the facts, fair and full analysis of the issues will serve to make clear to the disputants what it is they desire or contemn. The remarks which follow may be useful in suggesting the scope and direction of such an analysis.

There are some good reasons for believing that there is a "natural" tendency in a democratic society for the citizens to transfer responsibility for their economic security to the government. In a democracy there is always a struggle, open or concealed, between "those who have" and "those who have not." Only a small minority are able through hard work, skill, good fortune, or other means, to accumulate enough wealth to be free for the rest of their lives from concern about their economic security. The less fortunate majority, however, have the political power. It is unrealistic to suppose that this majority will not use their power to try to get more security. They have been taught that it is the function of a democratic form of government to promote the welfare of the people. It is unrealistic to suppose that they will not assume this to include their own economic welfare.

The citizens desire economic benefits; the politicians are willing to bestow them. The latter have but to vote tax money for this purpose; they do not have to earn it. In the beginning, comparatively few citizens will object to this, because, in a free enterprise society, the greatest part of the expense of social security is borne by those who have the largest income. The more extensive the government's social security program, the less the individual is dependent upon his own efforts. It also makes him less dependent upon his fellow citizens. Public unemployment compensation, for example, makes him less dependent upon an employer. If the compensation is unrestricted, he may even strike without too much economic loss, for the government pays most of the expense of his refusal to work.

How the transference of responsibility to the government will affect the sense of personal responsibility of the individual citizen cannot be accurately determined. In addition to the differences between individuals in respect to such personality traits as ambition, industry, and physical or mental energy, there are other variable factors which must be taken into consideration. There are the effects of established habits, social pressure, and education to be considered. The effects will certainly be different on those who "have less" than on those who "have more." It is likely that the effect on the individual will be proportionate to the extent of the benefits. If the government assumes only a small fraction of the responsibility for economic security, no sensible person will cease trying to provide for the balance. The way in which a man earns his living may have some influence. In the case of unskilled labor, work itself is not rewarding, only the wages earned by it. Reduction in the need for it is more than welcome. Even people who find their work interesting would be glad to have less of it to do.

In a capitalist society, social legislation enables the underprivileged to get something for nothing, or practically nothing, because they get it at the expense of the more privileged taxpayers. This, it is claimed, and with much justice, develops in the underprivileged individual the notion that the world owes him a living. It is bound to make the beneficiary less self-reliant and may well make him less industrious. The shiftless and improvident are likely to become more so. The facts seem to support the contention of the critics that social legislation tends to make citizens benefit-minded and that the demand for it is cumulative.

The facts also justify the contention that social legislation increases the dependence of the citizen on the government and therefore effects a change in his citizen-personality. His thinking, his motives, and his interests will all become more political. More and more of his life will be channeled through government bureaus and government officials. It may be argued that he can regain his independence whenever he wants to; but to believe this is to forget that, as a result of his increased economic dependence, he may gradually lose his interest in political independence. Human beings are not likely to worry much about their loss of political independence when their economic situation is being improved. It is by the promise of economic improvement that men have been persuaded to accept totalitarianism. If we accept totalitarian states as indicative, there is more reason for expecting unfavorable than favorable effects of the loss of economic independence on the spirit of liberty.

It is nevertheless quite likely that the danger of loss of the desire for political independence is exaggerated by the critics. There is no reason to suppose that the love of independence which accounted for democracy in the first place will disappear as completely as is assumed. The critics also forget the presence of a strong restraining influence in the democratic state, the strength of which increases concomitantly with the development of paternalism: those who have more economic security than they need will oppose social legislation which, in their opinion, goes far beyond the morally justifiable and socially necessary function of public care for the needy and the unfortunate. They will not object to contributing more to the upkeep of government than those who have less, but they will not care to do this for the purpose of supporting the lazy, the shiftless, and the irresponsible. To be sure, the more pessimistic among the critics will insist that these "rugged individualists" will be outvoted and gradually eliminated, or at least become thoroughly discouraged. Even in them the ambition to excel, or even to work more than necessary, will become atrophied.

One claim of the opponents of paternalistic legislation cannot well be denied, namely, that it will increase the complexity of government. Bureaucracy is a natural consequence of social legislation. The multiplication of bureaus and officials will result in duplication, cumbersomeness of operation, and interbureau rivalries. Bureaucrats tend to assume more and more power, even to usurp the power of the legislative branch of the government. The complexity of bureaus is likely to conceal this from the public and even from superior officials to whom this power properly belongs. Bureaucratic government easily becomes concealed government. The effectiveness of the essential democratic safety device of checks and balances will certainly be reduced. Lack of supervision will increase opportunities for favoritism and graft. The inefficiency natural to democracy will be greatly increased. The executive officials of the government will find it difficult to comprehend the complexities of government; the citizens will find it impossible. These dangers are serious dangers and believers in democracy will do well to reckon with them.

As to the ultimate outcome of the current struggle over so-called paternalistic legislation, no one can speak with certainty. Critics are justified in insisting that social security legislation has so far shown a tendency to create a demand for more. They are also justified in claiming that it is moving democratic government in the direction of socialism. What is really happening in the democratic world is a change in the traditional conception of the notion of individual responsibility. The truth of the matter is that in the United States, for example, a majority of the citizens think that they are entitled to more than they are now getting and that the surest and easiest way to get more is by social security legislation. A great number of citizens are interested only in the immediate benefits of this kind of legislation and are not giving one moment's thought to its political consequences. This is true also of some of the leaders of the economic and political groups which are favorable to this legislation, in whose case the motives for espousing this cause are strictly political in the narrowest and least favorable sense of the term. A few support the cause because they think that such legislation is furthering the cause of political revolution.

Both opponents and proponents of social welfare legislation should not forget that the contemporary trend to paternalism in government in the United States has developed in a free enterprise system. Certain characteristics of this system have obviously operated as predisposing conditions. These predisposing conditions are so well known as to require no more than identification here: accumulation of great private fortunes; industrial and financial consolidations representing tremendous wealth and power; huge profits; acquisition by economic wealth of political influence and power; and, above all, arrogant and ruthless use of wealth and power by those in control of it. Such concentrations of wealth and power were easily effected in the early and middle periods of the history of the United States. Because a great many citizens considered these characteristics unfavorable to the realization of their own ends, and because as private individuals they felt helpless to change these conditions, they became favorably disposed to what they considered remedial legislation. From this they were led in their thinking to the notion that it might be even better to abolish these conditions and to prevent their development in the future *by law*.

It is of course the voters who will largely determine what direction democratic government will take in the future. Universal suffrage is quite as much a potential means for limiting as for extending social security legislation. Opponents will either have to change the undesirable conditions which proponents of social security legislation are trying to remedy or they will have to convince the voters that these conditions are not undesirable, or that they cannot be escaped, or that their correction will result in even less desirable conditions. They will have to convince the voters that, if they wish to preserve the democratic form of government, the essential characteristics of the free enterprise system must be retained. Proponents will have to convince the voters that the preservation of the essence of democracy requires the kind of legislation which they advocate.

If the citizen hopes to distinguish between remedial and subversive legislation, he will need to keep before his mind the tenets which have been traditionally accepted as an essential part of the democratic faith, including the following: a democratic form of government should give the individual the greatest possible *opportunity* to satisfy his needs, desires, and interests, consonant with the assurance of this same opportunity to his fellow-citizens. The function of the government is to assure opportunity, not to bestow the benefits of the use of it. It is not a function of government to neutralize the consequences of irresponsibility. The individual citizen should not be relieved of all concern for the future economic security of himself and his family. Provision for future as well as present economic security should remain a matter of daily personal responsibility to the individual. On the other hand, the government should not permit some citizens to deprive others of the opportunity to attain economic security.

The government should also not deprive the individual of the opportunity to take better advantage of his opportunities than others are willing to take, and of the right to enjoy in consequence greater rewards than the less talented or the less industrious. The government should not remove incentives to excel by abolishing or neutralizing the rewards of intelligence, ambition, industry, and ingenuity. Nor should it limit the area of operation of private activity except as this is necessary to public safety and public welfare. It is the duty of the government to protect the private personality of the individual and to leave him his political independence. The citizen should give up as little freedom as possible; the government should deprive him of only so much freedom as is necessary. When the individual citizen thinks and acts, earns and spends, gains and loses only through the medium of government, he has ceased to exist as a *democratic* citizen.

\* \* \*

The dispute over the charge of lack of unity and continuity in a democracy is a good example of opposed evaluations of a form of government which result from a difference in conceptions of the purpose of government. What the critic calls disunity the proponent of democracy calls variety. According to the latter, difference is exactly what democracy is committed to preserve—difference in personalities, in satisfactions of needs, desires, and interests, and in ways and means by which men can attain their private and group ends—to the extent that this is compatible with common security and public order. The critics, on the contrary, hold it to be the function of government to establish as much similarity as possible. It is the function of government to make the individual conform to a conception of the citizen which, in their view, is categorically prescribed by their theory of government. The critics think in terms of the primacy of the state; the believer in democracy thinks in terms of the primacy of the individual. This is why the critics look upon the variety of a democratic society as proof of the failure of democratic government, whereas the believer in democracy hails it as a proof of its success.

The critics are so obsessed with standardization that they fail to discover the unity which underlies the variety which exists in a true democracy. They do not understand that the maintenance of variety is the unifying factor in a democracy just as the accomplishment of standardization is the unifying factor in a totalitarian state. Unity in variety is the democratic ideal, unity without tyranny and variety without chaos. It is the common purpose of the citizens to establish and maintain a practical balance between too much and too little freedom. This is what *unites* them as citizens of a democracy.

It is because they do not understand this that the critics misinterpret the meaning of some of the phenomena of life in a democracy. To the totalitarian critic, a national election in the United States looks like a complex of incipient political revolutions. The contradictory dogmatisms of political platforms, the dire predictions of the candidates, the violent charges and counter-charges and the organized enmity of political organizations seem to him an indication of hopeless disunity and an intimation of the early collapse of the democratic state.

He does not understand that all this fuss and fury is not a symptom of the desire to change the government but only of the desire to be elected. The purpose of the candidates is not to overthrow the government but to administer it. If he will observe closely, he will notice that, if there does happen to be a party which proposes a radical change in the form of government, all other political groups sooner or later combine against it. This does not mean that the citizens are at every moment clearly conscious of the underlying "philosophy" of a democratic election, that they are not often confused, and that they do not often work at cross purposes. It means that in every phase of genuine democratic living there is an underlying commitment on the part of all the citizens to cooperate in the realization of their private needs, desires, and interests and that this is the ideal which acts as the unifying bond between the individuals and groups; that it is this which prevents difference from engendering strife, variety from becoming chaos, liberty from becoming license, and government from becoming tyranny.

The critic also does not understand that this unity is not conceived as a stable condition which can be established once and for all. Both the character and degree of unity are in a state of flux. In critical periods of domestic adjustment, disagreement may become so general and so intense as to shake the confidence of even the firm believer in democracy. The strength of democracy, however, lies in the fact that it is committed to the principle of peaceful adjustment of even critical differences. Democracy provides the means for the constant readjustment of variety and unity. The attitude of the understanding citizen toward this process is like that of an engineer towards a delicate machine which regularly requires adjustment. The balancing of difference and agreement is politically a self-corrective process of social experimentation which is steadily pointed at the realization of the ideal of democracy.

The failure of some critics to understand the nature and purpose of this self-corrective process is also the source of the criticism that democracy lacks continuity. Democratic citizens are constantly seeking new ways of transforming disorganizing differences into cooperative aims. The purpose is always to preserve cooperation and tolerance. The purpose is to *preserve the peace*. The attempt to apply this policy in international relations, though actually a manifestation of continuity, is interpreted by critics as proof of a lack of continuity. The believer in democracy desires peace and he believes that it is attainable by means of this policy. He thinks that the democratic way is the way to peace. To the proponent of democracy, brute force is the great destroyer of continuity.

To nations and political leaders who believe in war as a legitimate instrument of foreign policy and to those who, though they condemn it, believe in its inevitability, the foreign policy of a democracy seems unrealistic, inconsistent, and impulsive. The general feeling is that, in a crisis, it is never certain what a democratic nation will do. The democratic love of peace and faith in its attainment offer one explanation of the apparent lack of consistency in the foreign policy of some democracies, a charge which has been particularly aimed at the people and government of the United States of America. In the case of the United States at least, there are other, and less favorable, explanations. In peacetime we have been too self-contained, too provincial, and too insular; a state of mind induced in part by our economic self-sufficiency, in part by our ignorance of the interests and purposes of other nations and other forms of government. We have been naive and much too trusting. We have had too much faith in the efficacy of our historic policy of avoiding foreign entanglements. Sudden shifts in foreign policy have sometimes been manifestations of political partisanship rather than of differences in principle and conviction. The lack of information and judgment on the part of the citizens about such difficult matters as foreign relations has enabled politicians from time to time to mislead great masses of the voters by misrepresentation of facts and by appeals to emotion and prejudice.

The confusion and discontinuity of our foreign policy have in general been a manifestation of a mixture or alternation of two attitudes which, though not necessarily contradictory, are not always esasily reconciled: an idealistic interest in international peace, and a realistic interest in national security; an interest in the welfare of the world, or some large part of it, and an interest in national advancement. One year we are granting large favors, and appeasing, and making concessions, the next year we are straining every effort to destroy the beneficiary of these favors. Our policy with respect to imperial ambitions and practices of foreign nations has also been inconsistent: in one case we support the maintenance of colonial domination and in another case we use all our influence to put an end to it. One moment we are romantic idealists; the next moment we are hardheaded realists. Foreign nations—including other types of democracies—cannot make sense out of these alternations of the national temper.

We can find excuses and explanations for these contradictions. For example, the foreign policy of a nation is not determined by that country alone; one nation cannot preserve the peace. In spite of excuses and explanations, no friend of democracy would care to conceal or minimize the weaknesses in our foreign policy. In an era of peace, much can be said for the educational value of difference of opinion on foreign policy. In an era when war is a constant threat, a nation must have internal unity and its foreign policy must have continuity. And it must make sense. There is a wide margin of safety in respect to domestic policy. When the external safety of a democratic nation is involved, however, this margin becomes very narrow and the dangers of disunity and discontinuity are very much greater. No nation, no matter how powerful and how resourceful, can hope always to meet international crises with a unity forced into being by an emergency and created for the occasion.

* * *

In striking a balance between the advantages and disadvantages of democracy, the critic, if he would be fair, must observe certain rules of objective analysis. The procedures of democracy can be evaluated only in the light of the purposes they are intended to serve. When so judged, it is clear that they are reasonably successful: the government fairly accurately and consistently reflects the needs, desires, and interests of the people. Because the ends of the government are a synthesis of private ends, its policies necessarily reflect the contradictions and confusions which exist among these private ends. The policies of the government are regularly a manifestation of competition between the ends of groups and classes of citizens for recognition. Changes in policy are reflections of changes in public opinion, the demand for which is motivated by the desire of the citizens for correction and improvement. The commitment of democracy to continued social experimentation implies the continued existence of imperfection and the unattainability of perfection.

Democracy reflects the strength and weakness of human beings. Just as an individual can live happily even though his thinking and acting life is full of contradictions, so a democratic state can exist and flourish in spite of the presence in its make-up of many contradictions. To be sure, these are much more obvious to the critics than to the citizens, for the latter have often rationalized them or become accustomed and insensible to them. The citizens, to be sure, make mistakes. This is inevitable. Kings and dictators also make mistakes. Since it is the governed who suffer from mistakes in government, no matter who makes them, why not let them make the mistakes to begin with? This puts both blame and consequences where they belong and will therefore make for the development of a greater and greater sense of responsibility.

Critical evaluations of forms of government must be comparative. Do democracies make more and greater mistakes than other forms of government? Where they have made mistakes, what has happened to the people? And to the form of government? Is not illegal lynching a lesser evil than legal liquidation? What is the difference between slavery, which the democracies abolished, and the labor camps which Soviet Russia has instituted? If we compare the (alleged) low level of universal education in a democracy with the high level of the selective aristocratic system in some European democracies, which is to be preferred? This being settled, how does the favored system compare in promise for humanity with the controlled system of education in Communist Russia? And how does life in general, as lived and as livable in a democracy, in all its phases, with all its potentialities and limitations, compare with life in an absolute monarchy or autocracy or fascist state, when considered in the light of the sum total of opportunities for the satisfaction of the needs, desires, and interests of human beings?

In times when problems of human relations are comparatively easy to solve and the form of government can safely be taken for granted, it is easy to believe in democracy. Loyalty is at such times little more than negative acceptance. But in times of internal or external crises, when democratic procedures are put to the test and the principles on which they are based are challenged, the citizen is forced to make a choice. At such times the citizen will have to strike his own balance between the virtues and faults of a democracy. How fairly and intelligently he will do this will depend upon the extent of his political understanding, not only of the virtues and faults of his own form of government but of non-democratic forms of government. When he has adjusted the balance, he will be in a position to decide which form of government offers the best way of life to him and his fellowmen.

*SIXTEEN*

# The Future of Democracy

BEFORE CONSIDERING THE PROBLEM OF THE FUTURE OF DEMOCracy, it is necessary to determine what kind of democracy we are talking about. As has been indicated, particular democratic governments are realizations of the basic principles of democracy in varying degrees of completeness. The ideal democracy, which exists only in the mind, is the perfect balance between chaos and tyranny; real democracies are approximations to that ideal. Any democracy which now exists or will ever exist will lie on one side or the other of that theoretical point of perfect balance. In some democracies, for example, the individual will have less, in others more freedom. Degree of approximation in any particular democracy to the ideal will also vary in time; for political practices must be to some extent adapted to the conditions which happen to obtain at a particular time in a particular democratic state. In short, there is a difference between democracy in theory and democracy in practice. That difference may be great or small, depending upon several conditions: the age of the democracy, the character of government officials, the temper of the citizens, the physical environment, the presence of enemies, internal or external.

The view of democracy presented in the previous pages is a mixture of democracy in theory and democracy in practice. The principal purpose was to identify the essential characteristics of the democratic form of government: those characteristics, namely, which differentiate it from non-democratic forms of government and which therefore are unique. To that extent, the study has been concerned with democracy in theory. But a consistent attempt has also been made to focus attention on a real democracy, namely the United States, as a point of concrete reference. Political practices and conditions and opinions in the United States have been used as examples of democratic theory transformed into action. It was intended by means of these examples to show that practices may vary considerably and sometimes even fail to realize the basic principles of democratic theory.

These examples have revealed some of the qualifying and inhibiting factors which enter the picture when democracy in theory is transformed into democracy in practice. Sometimes the citizens do not have as much power as they think they have; sometimes they fail to exert their power as fully as they might. The citizens by no means initiate all governmental policies. Frequently they do no more than accept them from their officials or their party leaders. Strong-willed and ambitious leaders sometimes sabotage the expressed will of the majority of the citizens. Powers properly belonging to one branch of the government are sometimes temporarily usurped by officials in another branch. Administrative bureaus sometimes exercise power in fact which they are not entitled to in theory. There are times when duly elected officials are more influenced by special interests than by the mass of the voters, when an "invisible government" develops within the government and exerts more influence on policies than the "will of the people." A firmly entrenched political party or political leader may actually accomplish a temporary usurpation of power which represents a shift of democratic government in the direction of autocracy. The personalities of leaders and the moods of the citizens have an important effect on the conduct of the government at any time, and thus on the extent to which democratic principles and procedures are realized in the government. It is the nature of democratic government itself which makes possible considerable variation in public opinion, in political precedures, and thus in public policy.

An ideal government, since it exists only in the mind, can

be peopled with ideal citizens and ideal public officials. Such a government therefore has a theoretical perfection which is unrealizable in practice. The democracy of the United States, like every other existing democracy, is peopled with real human beings. The theorist in his study can make his citizens vote and his officials rule in accordance with the ideal principles which he has created for them. The citizens of a real democracy vote as they please, in accordance with their own conceptions of their personal needs, desires, and interests. Even a citizen's conception of what is good for his fellow-citizens, his notion of the "public good," is a private notion of a particular human being. That notion will represent all the characteristics of a human point of view. It will be a composite product of selfishness and unselfishness, reason and emotion, knowledge and ignorance, objectivity and prejudice. Public opinion and the result of any election will thus be a grand composite expression of all the faults and virtues of all public officials and of all the citizens.

The imaginary citizen of the ideal democracy can be expected to think and act as an ideal citizen should, that is, in accordance with "right reason." To assume that the citizens of an existing democracy will do so is a mistake. It is not intelligent, for example, to assume that in the negotiation of a compromise every participant will act as a judge instead of an advocate. The way in which he presents his case will reflect his reasoning, to be sure; but it is certain that he will be using his reason to advance his own cause. Although we are only beginning to realize this, human beings are not nearly as rational as has sometimes been thought. Thinking itself is directed by non-intellectual elements of the human personality, by needs, desires, and interests, and by the emotions associated with them —ambition, envy, fear, hope, sympathy, etc. Some of these human motivations and emotions and thoughts are social and some are anti-social. When we learn more about the non-intellectual determinants of thought we shall know better how to educate and influence citizens and future citizens.

The proponent of democracy will do well to avoid idealizing democracy and the democratic citizen. The end-product of this will be a utopia, an ideal democratic state, which exists only in imagination. Preoccupation with this ideal will be poor preparation for understanding and evaluating a particular democratic government. It will lead to disappointment and disillusionment, and, if he undertakes to participate in democratic government, to frustration. It may tempt him in consequence to shift his allegiance to some other form of government. If, instead, in his thinking about democracy in theory he had kept steadily in mind the nature of real human beings and the actual conditions under which a democratic government must operate, he would have prepared himself for the inescapable imperfections to which governments as well as human beings are heir. By keeping his eye constantly on the real he would have known how to modify the ideal so as to be realizable. Realistically considered, democracy as a matter of fact provides for just those qualifying and inhibiting conditions by which the theorist is so much disturbed. It is the essence of democratic theory to provide a form of government which will make allowances for differences among men, differences in faults as well as in virtues. The best it hopes to do is to make men tolerant and cooperative, to effect adjustments and compromises, to establish a reasonable and enduring unity in variety, to make it easier for men to live at peace with one another. It is with this conception of democracy in mind that we turn to a consideration of its future.

\* \* \*

Only authoritarians, who base prediction on dogmatism, can prophesy with absolute confidence. The communist, for example, is absolutely certain of the survival of communism—or pretends that he is—because the world revolution of the proletariat is provided for in his theory. Others, who are limited to the evidence of experience, cannot be so sure. Any prediction concerning the future of democracy must be based on a comparison of theoretical promise and concrete fulfillment. The theoretical potentialities of democracy are to be found in its principles and processes and in various statements of the ends which it proposes to realize and the means which it prescribes. The realities of democracy are recorded in its history and in the current political scene. Since the record of democracy is not complete, and may never be, any prediction based on experience must necessarily be tentative. As to its theoretical nature, there is the undeniable fact that democratic government is by nature an experimental and adaptive process. It is questionable if any man can marshall before his judgment all the facts about democracy; it is certain that he cannot anticipate all the external circumstances in which the democratic process will have to operate in the future. He who would seriously undertake to predict concerning the future of democracy must identify the actual patterns of experience and behavior which the history of democratic governments reveals and compare them with those which the theory of democratic government is dedicated to establish and maintain. Even then he must assume that the patterns, and the circumstances in which they have developed, will remain reasonably constant. Whether or not democracy *will* survive, and in what form, are hypothetical questions. Reflections on the future of democracy are necessarily to some extent speculations; they must be made in the sense and spirit of this proposition: if people will behave democratically and if circumstances will be reasonably favorable, then democracy will survive.

Although history reveals no absolute laws to the believer in democracy as it does to the authoritarian, it does reveal certain fairly constant patterns of experience and behavior on the part of citizens and government of democratic states. These patterns are the result of the relationships which are characteristic of democratic society, relationships between citizens and groups of citizens, between them and their government, and between a democratic government and other governments, both democratic and non-democratic. These relationships, when measured in terms of the aims of democratic government, reveal characteristic and persistent virtues and faults. They have determined their share of the measure of past successes and failures and it may be justly assumed that they will do so in the future.

Human institutions, like human beings, can be injured or destroyed by internal and external forces. Among these internal forces are weaknesses which are native and which cannot be eliminated. In the case of democracy they constitute a calculated risk which the believer in democracy accepts as part of the bargain. In his view, they are compensated for by the benefits of democratic government. Weaknesses constitute no serious threat to democracy as long as men in their hearts desire its benefits. Native faults become compulsive of judgment only when the citizen no longer values the native virtues more than he abhors the faults, or when he loses faith in the power of the virtues to survive.

Towards faults which are not inherent but accidental the believer in democracy necessarily takes a different attitude. Such faults as corruption, graft, and demagoguery can in his opinion be controlled, though he will grant that they cannot be entirely or permanently eliminated. These demoralizing influences are not likely to become dangerous in view of the moral common sense of the people. Their influence will be offset by education; their spread and growth prevented by vigilance. The processes of democratic government themselves keep the citizens government conscious. Frequent political campaigns and elections keep the citizens not only informed of what is going on in government but also invite them to do something about it. Even those who are inclined to leave this business to their fellows are stirred up by candidates for political office and by the more politically minded citizens. Even the dull-minded are from time to time brought to realize that their interests are involved and that they must attend to them if they are to be considered in the policies and processes of government.

Regular participation in political action and discussion develops in the citizens a democratic political sense which enables them to judge when the delicate balance of liberty and restraint is disturbed, if only to the extent of suspecting that their own liberties are in danger. Political experience develops in the citizens alertness to practices and attitudes which threaten to circumvent or weaken or corrupt the democratic process. The saying, "Eternal vigilance is the price of liberty," becomes something more important than a handy quotation for patriotic occasions. It comes to be recognized as a statement of the reason why citizens vote. It identifies the only way in which the citizens of a democracy can protect themselves against forces which threaten to destroy the democratic state from within.

## The Future of Democracy

The uncertainty of prediction concerning the future of any particular democracy is enhanced by the fact that there is no way of accurately measuring these forces. Since the survival of an institution in a critical period depends upon the balance of the conserving and destroying forces operating within it, the student can do little more than assert this principle and identify the forces. He can feel certain with respect to a particular democracy that it will not survive if the citizens became insensible or indifferent to such destructive influences as official corruption, usurpation of power by the government, serious economic dislocations and injustices, etc. But he cannot be certain about the citizens. There is, for example, no accurate way of determining how many citizens of a democracy only tolerate it in the sense of accepting its benefits without actually believing in it. Not an inconsiderable number of people in every democratic nation look upon democracy as merely a transitory way of political life: their faith and their commitments have as their object a better (but undemocratic) form of government. There are forces at work in a democracy which have a tendency to encourage undemocratic ways of thinking and acting. These sooner or later create an unbalance by disturbing the equilibrium between freedom and restraint which it is the unique purpose of democracy to maintain. No one can tell whether at such a time the democratic sense of the citizens will or will not be keen enough to discover this danger. No one can predict in advance whether they will or will not have the desire and the courage to eliminate its causes. Among internal dangers, there is none so threatening and so insidious as the loss or surrender by the citizens of their political independence. With respect to this danger, the student of democracy can predict with confidence. This is the disease which, if not checked, is certain to be fatal. As a result of the failure to remain *self-corrective,* a democracy may become *self-destructive.*

\* \* \*

There is, to be sure, also danger from without. It has been said that "very few established institutions, governments, and constitutions . . . are ever destroyed by their enemies until they have been corrupted and weakened by their friends." This statement contains a warning which believers in democracy will do well to keep in mind. But they should not take the implied guarantee too seriously. The healthiest and most flourishing democracy can be destroyed by forces against which the most devoted believers are helpless. A democratic government, like any other form of government, must function in a setting. This setting may be far from ideal; it may even be definitely unfriendly. It must not be so unfriendly as to make positive adaptation to it impossible. A democratic government cannot survive every degree of environmental hostility. The believer may be convinced that, even if a particular democratic state or constitution is destroyed, democracy as such will arise again in some other place or time; but that conviction, though comforting, is not relevant. What he as a citizen of a particular democratic state must recognize is that there are external enemies which may destroy that particular state. Enemies are no respecters of governments. The citizen may wear his faith in the survival power of democracy as a shining shield; it will not make his government impregnable to an external enemy.

Democracy, as any other form of government, requires for survival a reasonably favorable economic environment. In one sense of the term, this is not part of the external environment at all but of the internal structure of the democratic state. A democratic form of government to a large extent creates its own economic environment. Its laws are important determining causes of the economic state of the nation. If their effects are unfavorable, the cause is internal and the enemy is within. There are other determinants of the economic health of a nation, however, over which a government has no control, no matter what its form. The physical resources of a nation are not inexhaustible. The development of a serious unfavorable ratio between physical resources and population is an "external" enemy and one of the potential causes of the downfall of a democratic government. Ruling out forcible seizure of the resources of neighbors, there are no means, currently acceptable, by which any government can prevent or fully compensate for the exhaustion of its essential physical resources. In spite of its obvious innocence and helplessness, the government may be held responsible by the citizens. To overthrow it is then a counsel of despair.

Economic crises in neighboring countries or in the world generally are other potentially dangerous external conditions. A sudden physical catastrophe, brought about by natural forces, whether localized within a democratic state or general in scope, is another kind of external enemy by which a democratic nation may be destroyed. Such external enemies are likely to "attack" any nation, no matter what its form of government. There is nothing in the character of democracy to make a democratic nation especially susceptible or defenseless with respect to such enemies. On the contrary, a good case could be made for the claim that a democracy, because of the strongly developed cooperative responsibility, self-reliance, and experience in self-government of its citizens, would be less easily demoralized and thus more resistant to such destructive forces.

The same claim could be made with respect to the danger represented by hostile neighboring nations. In spite of these potentialities, a democratic government is not likely to survive if it is attacked by an enemy which is determined to destroy it and has the power to do so. A democratic government must have a policy which takes full cognizance of the existence of such enemies. Fatalistic acceptance of whatever the future may bring is surrender before one is defeated. To become a militaristic nation is certainly foreign to the democratic temper, for militarism implies the abrogation of the basic democratic commitment to settlement of conflicts by compromise. Not to believe in war is not to abolish it, however. A democratic government and a democratic people must be prepared to fight as well as to compromise. The only safe policy is to assume that in the future there will be governments which will not believe in compromise or which will think that they can avoid the necessity of practicing it. The foreign policy of a democracy must include the principle and practice of realistic preparedness. Faith in peace is a pathetic fallacy if other nations believe in war. In a world in which powerful nations believe in force, democracy cannot afford to lead from weakness.

With respect to external enemies, the situation for democracies in the world seems never to have been so generally precarious as it is today. The reason for this is the fact that all democratic nations are collectively threatened. The existence of a ubiquitous and powerful anti-democratic movement represents a world crisis for democracy. The enemy is committed to the universal establishment of a form of government which is in several essential respects the direct opposite of democracy. In the foreign policy of communism, there is no provision for the existence of a democratic state. For the communist, the existence of a non-communist state anywhere in the world is not merely a potential danger; it is a moral evil. Any democratic state, no matter how small or how helpless, is a historical anomaly. It must transform itself or be transformed to conform with the dialectical process of history. Both theory and practice clearly reveal that believers in the communist form of government are committed to the abolishment of democracy.

The believer in democracy is under no such dogmatic compulsion. He has no desire to destroy other forms of government; on the contrary, he believes that any nation should be free to choose whatever form of government it desires. He is not opposed to political or any other cultural form of nationalism. As a matter of fact, he believes in the value and necessity of cultural diversity. Belief in individual diversity is one of his most basic and most cherished doctrines. And what is cultural diversity but individual diversity writ large! He believes that the democratic way of living together of the citizens of a nation can be established between nations. That is why he believes so strongly in the need of an international association of nations which will be itself a democracy. This is his answer to the communist and his solution to the current world crisis.

Will the communist choose this solution also? Many believers fear that he will not do so unless he is compelled by the failure of his own international policy. He would be foolish not to welcome the opportunity to develop his form of government in his own country in a setting of international peace and security. If he will give up his fanatical determination to make all the world communist, he will have no external problem of political survival. The believer in democracy is not planning forcibly to transform communism into democracy.

If the communist refuses the democratic solution and continues to pursue his present program of world conquest by force, he will plunge the world into a catastrophe, the

## The Future of Democracy

dimensions and consequences of which are almost beyond imagining. For believers in democracy are not going to submit peacefully. They are not committed to tolerance of attempts to destroy democracy. They, too, realize that there is no dependable alternative to a democratic ordering of international relations except war. If the communist states refuse to solve conflicts by conciliation, adjustment, and compromise, the democratic nations must necessarily accept the communist alternative.

No one can tell who will win this struggle. The only certainty is that the survivor will pay a cost so frightful that survival will be but a hollow victory. It seems certain that the post-war state of the participants in the struggle, both vanquished and victors, will be such as to prove that the means used to settle the conflict were stupid and wrong; that they were immoral from the standpoint of human dignity; that they were self-destructive instead of self-corrective from the standpoint of the advancement of civilization; that they were inconclusive rather than conclusive from the standpoint of what is politically best for mankind. A victory won by force does not prove which side offered the better way of life. For the believer in democracy, a victory for communism would certainly not prove that communism ought to survive but only that it did, this time, survive a test of brute force. The faith of the believer in democracy might be shaken but it would not be destroyed.

\* \* \*

This faith implies a conviction that it is democracy that *ought* to survive in this struggle. How does the believer in democracy justify this faith? This is a quite different question than whether or not it will survive. To begin with, since he believes that the authority of government comes from the consent of the governed, he believes that the governed are free to choose the kind of government they desire. Men are under no superhuman or extrahuman compulsion to choose this or that form of government. Under this freedom, a man, generally speaking, will choose that form of government which promises him the most favorable opportunity to live the kind of life which he desires to live. Contrary to the claims of authoritarians, this does not imply that the selection will be an arbitrary one and that therefore the consequences of this freedom of choice will produce chaos in human relations. It is true that democracy accepts variety in needs, interests, and desires among men as a primary datum. But this principle itself introduces an ordering principle; for the desire to satisfy these needs, desires, and interests is the unifying principle which limits the variety. The fact that men since the beginning of time have devised a variety of ways and means for effecting cooperatively the realization of their purposes is concrete proof of the operation of this ordering principle. The invention of various forms of political government is one of its manifestations. When we say that the kind of government which a man chooses will depend upon the kind of life he desires to lead, we intend to imply that all men, or at least the majority of men, are committed to choose some kind of government, that the need for government is a human need, and that this common need unites men in their efforts to devise acceptable forms of government. Because men have private interests in common they have a common interest in the promotion of these interests. A man's choice of government is therefore not a purely individual and arbitrary choice. It is determined by interests which he has in common with his fellowmen, by his discovery of this community of interest and of the necessity, or at least the wisdom, of cooperative promotion of these common interests.

It may be argued that this analysis explains why men choose to have some kind of government but does not justify the choice of any particular form of government. It does no more than define the purpose of government in general. The proponent of democracy claims that it does more than this: it gives him a basis for asserting the superiority of democracy over other forms of government. It justifies his preference for democracy and his faith in it. It justifies his claim that a democratic form of government, better than any other form of government, realizes the human purposes of government. The specific reasons for his preference have been outlined in more or less detail in the preceding pages. Let us by way of conclusion review them in summary form.

The believer in democracy affirms that a government exists for the sake of the citizens and not the citizens for the

# The Future of Democracy

sake of the government. This doctrine is based upon his belief in the primacy of the individual. The justification for this doctrine is the natural fact that every human being is a *person*. The purpose of his whole life is to realize his own potentialities. The need of the individual to be himself is the cause of his demand for freedom.

This demand for freedom he shares with other individuals. The realization of this community of interest with other individuals is the source of another discovery, the need and advantage of cooperation. Cooperation increases and improves the opportunities for self-realization. This social discovery is also a "natural" fact and thus a realistic basis for faith in democracy. Cooperation quickly teaches the individual the need of modification and limitation of his efforts at self-realization. This need is the source of the principle of restraint, the correlative of freedom. The individual sacrifices some liberty in return for a guarantee of opportunity. In its simplest form, this guarantee assures him personal physical safety and the opportunity to pursue his purposes in peace and security. It also enables him to order his life, to give it continuity, to introduce system into his activities, and thus to plan for the future.

The most systematic and extensive form which cooperation with his fellow men takes is the establishment of democratic government. He and his fellows elect representatives to establish the necessary forms and degrees of promotion and limitation of interests. These representatives and their appointees make laws and interpret and administer them, all with and by the consent of those who are to obey them. Thus a democratic government is a form of cooperative self-realization. The ideal is to impose only such limitations as are necessary to permit the greatest possible realization of the purposes of all the citizens. In return for control and restraint the citizens obtain certain advantages. Laws create rights and impose duties. Right and duty are natural and logical correlatives, just as are freedom and restraint.

The business of making laws is never completed because cooperative self-realization is a continuous process. Life changes, times change, people change, the environment changes. Democracy takes note of the reality of change and therefore provides for orderly and peaceful change in the laws. Democracy provides its own means for keeping government sensitive to changing conditions, to the need for the correction of mistakes, for the control of public officials, and for the improvement of ways and means of cooperative self-realization. The art of democratic government is never completely learned. The learning of past experience needs constantly to be checked with the evidence of present experience. Democracy is a continuing experiment in freedom. Democracy thus avoids the extremes and excesses of dogmatism and authoritarianism; its history is not a succession of passionate avowals and equally passionate denials.

Democracy provides social machinery for the continuous peaceful adjustment of differences. Except for the law of the jungle, this is the only alternative. Men must either compose their differences or remain enemies. They must work together or fight one another. In a civilized society there is no escape from the necessity of working together because there is no escape from living together. Said Robert Frost,

"Men work together, . . . .
Whether they work together or apart."

Men who will not live together in peace have no alternative but to try to destroy one another. If they desire peace, they must grant others the rights which they claim for themselves. This is the democratic conception of "lebensraum," not the authoritarian, which Bernard Berenson characterized as "communal cannibalism." It is indeed logical for those who believe in war to think of it as an instrument of world conquest and absolute world domination, for until these ends are accomplished there can be no peace. For the believer in democracy, war can be justified only as an instrument of social therapy, as a defensive measure against those who refuse to compromise and thus refuse to live cooperatively. War can be justified only as destruction in the service of construction. In the democratic way there is no destruction, only limitation. Compromise nourishes life, it does not destroy it. The democratic method of compromise represents cooperation in *self*-control. The compromising parties establish an authority over themselves and are thus committed to recognize it. Self-government is not a denial but a manifestation of individuality.

Faith in the soundness of the democratic process is strengthened by the fact that the application of the principle is extensible in both directions. An individual can order his life to some extent on this principle. Most individuals, whether they are aware of it or not, actually do so. The way of life which they ultimately adopt is in some degree the result of an accommodation among various needs, desires, and interests. Though there are types and moments of disorganization when forceful and dramatic decisions are necessary, the way to a rich and harmonious life is by adjustment and balance. Once accomplished, the result is an order and peace within the personality, both in inner experience and overt behavior, which is not easily disturbed by circumstance. The stable personality is one in which an adjustment has been made between the heart's demand for indulgence and the mind's demand for order. Though men are not yet fully convinced of it, nations, too, could learn to live and work together in the democratic way. It has already been abundantly demonstrated that nonpolitical institutions, large and small, can be organized and administered democratically. The same is true for associations of institutions, even when these are international in scope.

If construed in popular psychological terms, democracy might well be described as cooperative functioning of heart and mind, specifically, of a *good* heart and a *sound* mind. This more specific identification takes note of the fact that differences between heart and mind can be adjusted. Neither reason nor sentiment is given exclusive control. Neither is permitted to mislead the other. Democracy is neither exclusively a logical system of ideas nor a chaotic welter of feelings. It does not propose to give men everything because they want it, nor to deprive them of anything except for good reason. It is not misled by illusions of perfection, but it does not despair of attaining reasonable order. It honors the ideals of men but also acknowledges the realities within him and outside of him. It is toughminded but good-hearted.

There is much justice in the complaint made by lovers of

dogmatic certainty that democratic theory cannot be reduced to a system of ideas, nor democratic practice to a code of rules. To some extent, democracy is in theory nothing more definite than a determination to live peacefully, and in practice nothing more than a continuous experiment in doing so. To live the democratic way efficiently and consistently is to live in the *spirit* of democracy. This spirit represents an integration of private conviction and public tolerance. It means to hold faithfully to one's own beliefs without implying contempt for those of others; to be privately certain without insisting that others are absolutely wrong; to respect one's own institutions without manifesting disrespect for those of others; to will to live one's own life consistent with goodwill to others.

To maintain a democratic society, men must live in the spirit of democracy. If men think and act in this spirit politically, they will provide themselves, through their government, with the most favorable environment possible for the pursuit of the good life, in the private as well as in the public sense of the term. As John Buchan put it in his autobiography, democracy "provides a fair field for the good Life, but it is not itself the good Life." In a democracy, it is possible to live several versions of the good life, in fact, more versions than can be lived under any other form of government without endangering peace and order. Democracy makes this possible because it seeks to maintain a reasonable balance between opposite forces. If these forces are over-indulged, they seek to destroy one another. If they are controlled, they function cooperatively. Democracy is the middle way; the middle way between chaotic individualism and authoritarian order; between license and tyranny; between traditionalism and opportunism; between dogmatism and experimentation; between sentimentalism and logic. The middle way is the reasonable way. On it, a man can walk with his fellows in peace and in dignity. On it, he and his fellows can practise the art of living together. Whether mankind will choose this way or not, no one can say. But the believer in democracy is convinced that he will be foolish if he does not do so.